THE TREE BRIDGE

DR. SHERRY L. MEINBERG

ISBN 978-1-959895-31-2 (paperback)
ISBN 978-1-959895-30-5 (ebook)

Printed in the United States of America

WESTPOINT
PRINT AND MEDIA

Dedication

To all of my students across the years,
that I have been lucky enough to know:
I hope you continue to celebrate *all* your successes,
big and little, one by one by one.
Hug a tree for me!

Trees can feel and respond
to pressure waves.
So trees can feel your hug,
and respond to your voice.

"The capacity to learn
is a gift;
The ability to learn
is a skill;
The willingness to learn
is a choice."

—Brian Herbert

"The beautiful thing
about learning is
nobody can take it
away from you."

—B.B. King

Contents

Chapter 1

THE STORM

Crash! Boom! Crackle!
Lightning slashed as thunder roared, and the wind howled, as sheets of rain pounded the roof.

"Oooooh!" the students moaned together, in appreciation, and in fear. The scene they were witnessing through the wall of classroom windows was beautiful, and scary, at the same time. Shock and awe.

The weather was so dramatic that Ms. Matson had pulled the blinds all the way up to the ceiling. She also turned off the classroom lights, the better to see this unusual happening. The children sat in the darkness and witnessed together this most unusual experience. Every now and then, lightning sparks illuminated the sky, followed by a deep roll of thunder. The storm raged on, as the noise of the rain hammering on the roof drowned out all speech.

Southern California is known for its sunny, calm days. And for most years, rain is a rare experience. It comes and goes so quickly, there is very little to remember about it. But this year was different! Toward the end of January and a couple of weeks in February brought two spectacular storms back-to-back. The ground was so saturated that the cleanup lasted for weeks and weeks and weeks! It was a statewide event, as 35 of the 58 counties were declared disaster areas.

No one had ever seen such a sight before. The newspapers and TV coverage were all gloom and doom. Every evening the children heard of a new catastrophe, which was discussed in class the following day. Thundering mudslides either crushed homes or completely filled them up with mud. Hurricane winds uprooted thousands of trees, and blew fences, roofs, and small wooden buildings apart. Raging waters swept many vehicles away. A dam collapsed, causing even more flooding. Five bridges washed out, stranding many families. Wild animals escaped from the zoo, causing widespread concern. Corpses floated away from a cemetery, which startled those who found the bodies. A landslide caused an entire mountain community to vanish overnight. The destruction of property was immense, at around 400 million dollars. Thousands of homes were without power or phones. Seven hundred families were suddenly homeless. There were 50,000 evacuations. Hospitals were overflowing, but luckily, only thirteen people died. It was no wonder why everyone was so frightened!

Just getting to school each morning was an adventure. Trees, bushes, downed power lines, and disabled cars were constantly clogging the streets and sidewalks. Junk was scattered everywhere. Luckily, most of the students lived nearby, in the surrounding neighborhood. It was easier for them to get to school, even though it was like a giant obstacle course. They had to climb over, under, and around various debris. Sometimes they had to backtrack, and take another street. It took them three times as long to arrive at school, and everyone was totally drenched when they got there, as the rain blew sideways under their umbrellas. All agreed that life would be a lot easier if they just wore their swimming suits to school.

Most of the teachers, however, lived a great many miles from the school, some in faraway cities. They had to deal with numerous detours. And each day, the detours were *different*, so they could never plan ahead. Sometimes the water was so deep at street intersections that the cars could not go through. Many vehicles stalled, and became stranded, until tow trucks could save them. Those unlucky teachers who had to drive from other cities had added difficulties and dangers to their morning drive. Sometimes they didn't show up at all. (This was before cell phones or email.) Accidents happened often, causing vast traffic jams and long waits. All the cities in the Southern California area were in deep trouble, with no end in sight.

The students were badly frightened. So whenever the subject came up, no matter what they were studying, the class would stop and discuss the situation. Everyone voiced their concerns. The children were pleased to know that they weren't the only ones who were scared.

They talked about the importance of having friends at a time like this. They talked about the importance of cooperation and helping others. They talked about the importance of maintaining a positive mental attitude in times of emergencies. But mostly, they talked about how scared they were, which seemed to bring a sense of oneness to the group. It was a comfort to the children, to see that they were not alone.

Chapter 2

DRYING OUT

Finally, at long last, the rains stopped, and the winds died down. Cleanup for the city was supposed to take another three weeks, but it took much, much longer than that. Locally, over 500 trees were toppled. It took a long time for the workmen to chop them up, and remove them.

The students were tired of being stuck indoors, and were glad that they could finally go outside for recess. The playgrounds were still too waterlogged to do much of anything, other than to just stand around. But it was great to be outside the classroom walls. And the air smelled so fresh and clean. The smog had yet to return.

Even though the thunder, lightning, and heavy rains had stopped, there were still some leftover winds to deal with. Everyone was tired of it all. Their energy levels were low, with a general attitude of dissatisfaction. So, at the point when most things had pretty much dried out, Ms. Matson took the class to Goldenrod Park.

They were going to see how much damage had been done to their local park. The third graders in Room 21 were used to going every Friday afternoon, where they could play with their friends from other third grade classrooms. The children always looked forward to these times in the park. They had the opportunity to be free to just *be*.

All of the boys and girls in the neighborhood liked to go to the park. But it was strictly off limits. Parents would never allow their children to play there, because of the gang influence. The teenagers took over the park in the late afternoons and evenings. And then, Goldenrod Park became loud, rowdy, and rough. So parents decided that the park was not safe. They did not consider those particular teenagers to be good examples for their children. And rightly so!

That meant that the large amount of playground equipment went unused for years. Until, that is, the third grade teachers decided to take their students to the park, in groups, together. And not just for safety reasons. They also wanted to give their students the opportunity to interact with each other, as well as play on the swings, bars, slides, and merry-go-rounds. All of the children looked forward to going to Goldenrod Park. The city's park playground equipment was different from that of the schools, and the children liked the change. It was great fun!

Chapter 3

GOLDENROD PARK

The students were quiet, as they tried to understand the destruction around them. The looks on their faces showed their disbelief. Giant trees were scattered everywhere, looking like a game of pick-up sticks. Huge bushes rolled around like tumbleweeds. Trashcans and benches were overturned. Litter was everywhere. Their beautiful park was destroyed. They had seen the damage on TV, but seeing it in person was shocking. They realized for the first time, just how strong Mother Nature can be.

Ever on the alert for an unexpected lesson, Ms. Matson decided to give the class a hands-on experience regarding the parts of a tree. She had them play Follow-the-Leader, winding around the fallen trees and bushes.

They stopped at the largest tree. It was *huge*. It was *massive*. It was hard to believe that trees could grow so big. Everyone oohed and ahhed over the size of it. They were amazed at the size of the roots, which were even bigger than the treetop. The tree had fallen in such a way that it looked like a giant bridge across the sidewalk.

Ms. Matson decided to lead the children up through the gigantic root system, across the trunk of the tree, and through the branches and leaves of the treetop, to jump off at the crown. She thought it would be an easy way to learn the parts of a tree, and that the experience would be great fun.

14

But the tree was much too big. It was way too high. The class looked at her bug-eyed with surprise. Very few wanted to try. It was just too scary to even think about!

"Uh-uh!" Many shook their heads from side to side.
"Nope!" others said, crossing their arms.
"No way!"
"Not me!"
"Never happen!"
"I can't do that!"
"I don't *want* to do that!" stepping backwards.

"How do you know?" Ms. Matson asked. She couldn't understand why her students weren't jumping at the chance to walk the length of the tree. She thought that it would be a wonderful experience for them. "You'll probably never have this chance again in your whole lifetime!" she urged. "Don't let this unusual opportunity pass you by!" Still, few wanted to try. Heads were rapidly moving back and forth.

"Now don't let the Worry Wolf get to you! Think positive!" she advised. But the class wasn't going for it. "Don't let the Worry Wolf huff and puff at your door!" Silence.

Ms. Matson tried again. "If you are comfortable all the time, you'll miss out on the chance to stretch and grow. Think of this as an *adventure!*" she said. "You are just like Indiana Jones!" Everyone's eyes perked up. "You are on a volunteer mission! You are the only ones who can save the little kindergartners that the mean old dragon stole! It is up to *you* to save them!" Everyone's imagination took hold.

"You must face your fears! Remember, you cannot grow without *challenges!*" Everyone loved to hear Ms. Matson when she talked like this. "*Participate* in life! It takes strength and courage to face what you fear! Now is the time for action!"

"YESSSS!" shouted some of the boys.

15

DR. SHERRY L. MEINBERG

"Onward and upward!" shouted others, repeating Ms. Matson's favorite words.

"Let's do it!" shouted Jax, starting to climb up the roots, setting an example.

"Come on!" shouted Hayden, motioning with his arm, as he followed Wyatt. "We must save the little kids!" Others immediately followed with comments of their own.

"The little kids need us!"

"*We can do it*!"

"No mean old dragon is going to stop us!"

"Aieee!"

There was a flurry of activity, as most everyone ran toward the fallen tree. A few hung back, of course, starting to look panicky. Ms. Matson was quiet, watching to see what the children would do. She wanted to see what they would decide for themselves. She always said that everything in life is a *choice*. Everyone knew that Ms. Matson would never force anyone to do anything that they were not ready for. So, the decision was up to them.

The more athletic boys and girls went first. They climbed up through the tremendous root system, and walked single-file along the tree trunk. They were surprised at how high they were off the ground. Jax and Hayden jumped off the crown of the tree, and ran back to the root system. They began helping the rest of the children to climb up, and have a turn. Wyatt and Jay stayed where they jumped off. They held up their arms and grabbed the hands of the other children, as they were about to jump off. Everyone was giving encouragement and prodding to those who needed it.

"It's fun!"

"You'll like it!"

"Come on! You can do it!"

"It's easy! You'll see!"

"Let me help you!"

Ms. Matson was delighted to see how the students were assisting each other. "Concentrate! Focus! Pay attention," she advised. "Just one step at a time…" She continued supporting their efforts by saying things like, "Simply put one foot in front of the other," "Trust yourself," and "You can do it!"

"Remember, your brain believes what you say!" she said. "To be a champion, you have to believe in yourself! Remember the story about *The Little Engine That Could*, by Watty Piper? Many of the children began chanting, "I think I can! I think I can!" While others began to chant, "I know I can, I know I can!" as they giggled and laughed together. And, the children that had already crossed the Tree Bridge, shouted, "I thought I could, I thought I could, I thought I could!"

Ms. Matson smiled and called out, "That's the spirit!" as she encouraged them, step by step. "Now and now, and now," holding hands with some of the girls, who were afraid, but wanted to walk the tree trunk. She wanted them to feel safe, when trying something new. "Remember, courage is like a muscle. It gets stronger with practice. Stretch yourselves!"

Some students had originally crossed the tree in a sitting position. They had inched along on their bottoms, using their arms and hands to move themselves along. Others crawled along on their hands and knees. "Remember," Ms. Matson said, "It doesn't matter where you start. It's where you finish that's important!" Several children had very creative ways to cross the Tree Bridge. Everyone applauded their efforts. Ms. Matson held the hands of some that were unsteady, and she slowly walked on the ground, while they walked the trunk.

At first, Riley, Mandy and Emily, held each others' hands, and crossed the tree bridge sideways together. They carefully slid their feet across the bark. Later, they were able to let their shoes leave the safety of the wood. Finally, they could walk across it alone, without help, balancing perfectly. After jumping off the end of the tree, the three girls grabbed each other's hands. They squealed as they jumped up and down together. Then they danced around in a circle. They were so happy! Everyone giggled and laughed with them.

"We did it!"

"We saved those little kids!"

"Yeah, those cute little kindergartners…"

"That mean old dragon didn't stop us!"

"Yes! You all took the challenge, and you accomplished your goal! Allow yourself to feel *good* about your achievement!" praised Ms. Matson. It was a joyous occasion. They had conquered their fears. They felt a sense of accomplishment, and did a little happy dance like Charlie Brown's dog, Snoopy. The class laughed, as they repeated the words their teacher liked to use.

"Practice makes perfect!"

"Trust yourself!"

"You never know what you can do 'til you try!"

Ms. Matson had a silly grin on her face, as they danced around her.

"Have you noticed that when you do something new, you feel braver and stronger in other areas, too?" asked Ms. Matson. The students nodded their heads in agreement. Some shook their clasped hands over their heads. Others thumped each other on their backs. Several gave the thumbs-up sign. And they happily slapped high-fives and low-fives all around. They felt so good about themselves. "Feel how much energy you have… how alive you feel…," she said. Ms. Matson always wanted them to celebrate their successes.

Everyone circled around and around the tree, going faster and faster. Their faces beamed. They were filled with pride. When the students became satisfied that they had conquered the Tree Bridge, they finally got tired of the game. And their interests took them elsewhere. They broke up into smaller groups, to explore and investigate the park on their own.

Ms. Matson sat down on a bench, and watched her third graders. Some played on the equipment. Some molded the damp sand into tunnels and roads. Others played hide-and-seek. A few of the girls skipped around singing out loud, "If you're happy and you know it, clap your hand, CLAP, CLAP…"

A bunch of the boys were excited to discover that the bark of one fallen tree had split wide open upon crashing. The inside of the old tree was filled with one humungous beehive. That sure got everyone's attention! The honeycomb was tremendous. A lively class discussion followed. Everyone made buzzing noises, since no bees were found. They worried about what happened to the bees. There was more than enough of the honeycomb for everyone to have a large chunk, to take home to show their families.

Others started rolling the big bushes into one place. They made an enormous bird's nest. The children's imaginations took over again. They pretended that their nest had fallen from the high branches of the Tree Bridge, when it had crashed in the storm. Finally, the rest of the class saw what their classmates were doing, and came to join the fun. The class decided that they were a large family of birds. Everyone flapped around, flying here and there, swooping everywhere, cawing to each other. It was a great way to leave the park that day: as a *family*.

Chapter 4

THE APOLOGY

The first thing next morning, Ms. Matson said, "Class, I have something to say to you about yesterday's Tree Bridge adventure." Everyone leaned forward to hear what she was going to say. She sounded so serious.

"First, I want to thank you for reminding me that everyone doesn't think the same way I do. Sometimes I forget," she said. "Thank you for reminding me," she smiled, nodding at the group. "And second, I want to apologize, because you are so important to me." *What is she talking about?* the children wondered to themselves. Many had confused looks on their faces.

"Let me explain myself," she began. "When I was your age, I *loved* walking on fences. It was considered a fun thing to do! Whenever my friends and I ran out of things to play, we would always enjoy walking on top of the old wooden fences. We played Follow-the-Leader on everyone's fences in the neighborhood, all the time." Everyone liked hearing Ms. Matson's stories. They were all listening carefully.

"So I thought that *you* enjoyed the same thing. I couldn't understand why you were so reluctant to walk across the tree trunk," she said. "I kept thinking that it was just the same as walking across fences. Only just a little higher. I thought about it all evening. And, *finally*, I understood what the problem was." She paused, as she looked at all her students.

They waited quietly, wondering where she was going with all these words. They didn't understand what she was talking about, but that was alright. The *feelings* mattered, more than the words.

"I realized that you had *never* had any practice walking fences, because your fences aren't the same kind as the fences of my youth," she continued. "Just like everything else in life, fences have changed, too." Soft laughter was heard around the room.

"Last night, in my mind's eye, I pictured your neighborhood. I realized that some of you had chain-link fences around your houses. And chain-link fences cannot be walked on. Others of you have iron bar fences around your houses, and iron bar fences cannot be walked on. Still others of you have cinderblock walls. These, of course, *could* be walked across, except that most of these walls have ivy or other vines growing on top of them. And, some of you live in apartments, so you have no fencing at all." Everyone smiled and nodded. They were glad she had figured it out.

"It's always hard to try something for the very first time," she continued. "Especially if you haven't even seen it done before. And it's even harder if other people are *watching* you, because you don't want to make a mistake in front of them. No one wants that!" Heads bobbed back and forth in agreement. No one likes to make a mistake in front of other people."
    "You got that right!"
    "You can say that again!"
    "It's too embarrassing!"

Ms. Matson was quiet for a minute. "So I want to apologize to you, for putting you all in that position. No wonder it was so scary for you! You had no experience in fence-walking." The students immediately responded at the same time.
    "Oh, that's alright!"
    "But we did it!"
    "That's okay, Ms. Matson!"
    "Don't feel bad!"
    "Everyone walked the Tree Bridge!"

"It was FUN!"
"We all learned how…"

"Thank you for trying to make me feel better," she continued. "I just want you to know, that if ever something like this happens again, please tell me that you've never done it before. Tell me that it is a new experience for you. *Communicate!* How is anyone going to know how you *feel*, unless you tell them? Otherwise, you might find yourself in this kind of situation again. And that will be like putting the cart before the horse."

"What does that mean?" everyone demanded, giggling together. *Here she goes again, using strange sayings*, thought several students.
　　"Is that another *idiom*?" asked Riley.
　　"Is that another old expression?" asked Emily.
"Soooo glad you asked," said Ms. Matson, wiggling her eyebrows at them. "Yes, you are right. It is another *idiom*…" She walked over to the chart rack, and flipped through the charts until she found the Idiom Chart.

"Picture in your mind's eye: a wagon with a horse behind it. Have you all imagined it?" she asked.
　　Yesss!" said the class.
"Can the horse pull the wagon this way?"
　　"Noooo!" laughed the class.
"You are exactly right. So the old saying 'Don't put the cart before the horse,' means don't put things in the wrong order. First things first. Don't reverse the order, or mix up the order of things." Ms. Matson wrote the saying on the chart.

"Everything in life is best learned in stages," she explained. "You take small steps and celebrate each successful step you take. In other words, you learn to crawl before you stand, and you learn to walk before you run. You have lots of practice with each skill, before you try learning a harder skill. You start with the easy things first." Heads nodded around the room.
"Does a baby suddenly run races?"
　　"Noooo!" Everyone laughed at the very thought.

"You wouldn't be expected to know how to read, if you'd never seen the alphabet before, would you?"

"Noooo!" yelled the class.

"You wouldn't be expected to do algebra or geometry—very advanced math—if you'd never learned to add and subtract, would you?"

"Noooo!" yelled the class.

"You wouldn't be expected to paint masterpieces if you'd never dabbled with art before, would you?"

"Noooo!" yelled the class.

"You wouldn't be expected to compose music, if you never learned to sing a song, would you?"

"**Noooo**!" yelled the class, as they laughed. These examples were just too silly.

"So the old saying, 'Don't put the cart before the horse,' simply means that you shouldn't do things backwards. First things first. A baby drinks from a baby bottle before it learn to drink from a cup!" Everyone laughed again. They all had stories of baby brothers or baby sisters learning to eat and drink by themselves. What a mess!

"What I'm trying to say is that you should have had lots of practice before you attempted to cross the Tree Bridge. You could have possibly walked a low balance beam, or a fallen log on the ground, first. Then you might have practiced walking around the wooden edges of the sandbox, which is about a foot off the ground."

"Then you could have had practice walking the tops of sawhorses, which are much higher. Then later, perhaps, you could have walked across brick walls, which are much higher off the ground. You should have had practice balancing on increasingly higher objects, before you ever tried to cross that high Tree Bridge." Ms. Matson shook her head. "So, you didn't take any baby steps, you all took a giant leap!"

"Uh-huh!"

"That's right!"

"We leaped, that's for sure!"

"Yep! We did it!"

"One giant leap for mankind!" quoted Jax, as everyone giggled.

"I didn't realize until late last night, how truly frightening it must have been for you, being so high off the ground. And I am very sorry to have put you through that experience…"

"But we did it!"

"We succeeded!"

"It was fun, after we learned how…"

Everyone nodded their heads in agreement, with bright smiles on their faces.

"I think you all know that safety was not a problem. I would never have placed you in harm's way. I think you all figured out that the branches of the tree were large, and slanted down in such a way, that if anyone had fallen, you wouldn't have been hurt. You would have only softly, gently, rolled down the long branches," Ms. Matson continued. Nodding heads were seen all around the room.

"I am bringing this all to your attention because I want you to know that your success in walking across the Tree Bridge was much more of an achievement than you think it was! It was a very BIG victory, because you hadn't practiced anything similar beforehand, and it was *scary*!" Ms. Matson clapped her hands for them, and the class joined in. "Now, give yourself a pat on your back, for a job well done!" And they did.

"In the future, when you come across a problem that you feel you can't handle, think back to the time when you were in the third grade. Think back to the time when you crossed the Tree Bridge by yourself." Ms. Matson tapped her head. "Know that you can succeed at anything you set your mind on! After all, you've already proven it to yourself."

Everyone was trying to make Ms. Matson feel better. They were not used to anyone apologizing to *them*. After all, they were just kids. But it made them all feel better, to know how much she cared about them.

"I appreciate your concern," Ms. Matson said. "But it is important to apologize when you think you have done something wrong, or if you've made a mistake, or acted badly." She paused. "It's important to tell people how you *feel,* and ask for forgiveness. So I am. I am apologizing to all of you. Please do me the honor of accepting my apology."

"Thank you for your apology," everyone said in various ways, using their best manners. Wow! Ms. Matson treated them like real people. Like grownups! She always considered their feelings. That's one of the reasons they loved her so much.

Chapter 5

PROJECTS

Over the next several days, the students wrote a number of stories. It was not surprising that all had trees or Tree Bridges in them. The whole class enjoyed hearing these tales of hair-raising thrills and high-speed adventure: tales of action, heroism, and courage.

The students were soon to choose their tree projects, as they had done with other subjects during the year. It was always fun, because each one got to be the teacher. They had done this many times before, so they weren't scared or embarrassed anymore, standing in front of the group to share what they had learned. They actually looked forward to it.

Although the subject of trees was clearly on everyone's minds, the students weren't too sure there was a whole lot more to learn about them. After all, trees were just a big plant, with a stick up the middle. They had lived around trees for all their lives. And, they learned things about trees in the first and second grades. How much more could there possibly be to learn? *Not much*, they thought.

"Now don't get discouraged. Remember, what I've told you before," said Ms. Matson. "Learning is like a spiral. Each year, you learn a little more in school about subjects that you already covered in lower grades." She drew a gigantic spiral on the chalkboard. "Each year, you add more knowledge to what you already have," she soothed. "There is always more to learn." Her spiral looked like a giant tornado, as everyone laughed.

The class didn't look convinced, however. "Believe me," she said, smiling at them. "I think you will surprise yourselves by how much new information you will find. And, anyway, you can always discuss things that you already know, because others may not know exactly what you know. You may have been in different schools, with different teachers, who don't teach the same way. And don't forget: You can get information not only from books, and TV, but also from your parents and other family members, or your friends and neighbors. Even a friendly librarian might help you. We don't care where you get your information from, we just want to learn from *you*."

Every now and then, students *did* have questions, and Ms. Matson added the questions to a class chart. "Maybe someone will find an answer to some of our questions.

THINGS WE'D LIKE TO KNOW ABOUT TREES

1. **Do trees talk to each other? How do they communicate?**
2. **Do different tree species get along?**
3. **Do trees have any enemies?**
4. **Do trees know what is going on around them?**
5. **What makes trees sick?**
6. **Do trees sleep? Dream? Count?**
7. **Do trees sweat?**
8. **How do trees know when it is autumn, winter, spring, or summer?**
9. **Do trees ever get afraid? What scares them?**
10. **Trees just stand around doing nothing. Do trees have a boring life?**
11. **Do trees like people? Do they like kids?**

Over the next few days, the students chose the subjects they wanted to work on. Then they set about finding material for their projects. In a couple of weeks, they were ready to share their projects. Some wanted to be first (to get it out of the way, so they could relax), and some wanted to be last (to give them more time to finish their reports).

The third graders looked forward to hearing each other's speeches. Some would be long, and some would be short. But that didn't matter. Everyone researched as much as they could, and got help from as many people as they needed. They were eager to share what they learned, and would tell Ms. Matson when they were ready. Ms. Matson always said, "It's not what you know, it's what you *do* with what you know, that counts. And you'll be sharing your knowledge with others. If you each learn a little bit, and share your knowledge with others, then everyone learns a lot!"

Chapter 6

TREE SPECIES

Hayden came to the front of the classroom. His poster was very simple. It had the word TREES on it, and he had quickly drawn a few trees. Art wasn't his focus. He spent his time getting information. He was just introducing the subject, reminding the class of what they might already know, and adding a few new facts, here and there. But he couldn't wait to share.

"There are more than *73,000* different species of trees around the world!" he bellowed. No one could believe it! Everyone started giggling, and rolling their eyes, because Hayden was so excited. **"And scientists say there are at least 9,000 more, to be discovered!"** Hayden was really thrilled to share what he had discovered about trees.

"We know that trees are plants. They are *woody* plants. Their trunks, limbs, branches, and twigs are their stems. We know they have seeds, roots, and leaves, just like other plants. The main difference between trees and regular plants is that trees are bigger. And because they are bigger, they have to have thick, woody trunks to hold them up. A skinny little plant stem just couldn't to the job of holding up all that weight.

"There are some trees that are called *Pioneer Trees*," as Hayden pulled out his notes and read, "like white birches, willows, aspens, poplars, pine, oak, cedar, and hickory. Pioneer Trees are the first trees to settle in sites that were damaged by wildfires, floods, storms, landsides, or clear cuts. (Clear cuts mean that lumberjacks had cut down all the trees in one area). Pioneer Trees improve the dull, poor soil, in unused areas by their deep roots, which improves the soil, and prevents soil erosion. They grow fast, and then they produce a vast amount of seeds. Pioneer Trees bring shade for birds and animals, and they slow down the winds. And because Pioneer Trees are the first trees, they encourage insects, birds, and animals to move into the area.

"Trees come in all sizes. Some are small trees, just a few inches tall, like this Bonsai tree." Like a magician, he pulled a cloth off a little tree on the table, as everyone oohed and ahhed, and made comments. He held the container up higher for everyone to see. "These trees are very popular in Japan. The meaning of the word Bonsai is "tree in a pot." Everyone got the giggles again. "Bonsai trees have been around for thousands of years." Many of the students had never seen a Bonsai tree before, and couldn't believe how tiny it was. "Like miniature trees," they whispered.

"There is also another tiny tree called the Dwarf Willow, that lives in the bitter cold and deep snow. It hugs the ground, so the powerful winds won't fly it away. It takes **100 years** to grow just eight inches tall." Hayden held up a ruler, so everyone could see how little it grew in a whole century. No one could believe it.

"We see mostly middle-sized trees, although they seen very big to us. But there are many larger size trees that are *huge*! We will probably see them only in pictures. These are the *giants* of the plant world. There are over 100 species that grow over **200 feet tall**."

"Oh, my goodness class," Ms. Matson interrupted. "I am a little over five feet tall. So, it would take over **40** of me, stacked on top of each other, to be as high as those trees! *Can you believe that?*" The class laughed, having trouble visualizing 40 Ms. Matsons all together. It was just too funny.

"Trees are the largest living things in the whole wide world!" Hayden boomed. That sure got everyone's attention.

Several called out, "Bigger than whales?"

Yes!" Hayden answered.

"Bigger than dinosaurs?"

"Yes!" Hayden answered. "Even the biggest dinosaur wasn't even close to an average-sized tree. These trees are huge, enormous, *gargantuan!* The students were quiet, thinking about that.

"There is one special tree named the Howard Libbey Tree. It is in the Redwood National Park, in California. It is almost 368 feet tall!"

"Oooooh!"

"That's 63 feet taller than the Statue of Liberty!" he exclaimed.

"Wow!" responded the class. That sure put a picture in their minds! They had recently studied all about the Statue of Liberty, so they knew how big she was.

"And one of the *heaviest* trees is the giant sequoia (which is also in California). One is named the General Sherman. Although lightning knocked off its crown, it is 30 stories tall, and weighs over **two million pounds**!"

"Ooooh!"

"Two million?"

"Pounds?"

"That doesn't seem possible!"

"One of the tallest trees to be discovered, so far, was one that was living in Australia. When it finally fell, down, it made a bridge across a wide canyon..."

"Just like our Tree Bridge!" several said, as everyone looked at each other in amazement.

"Just like Indiana Jones uses," smiled others.

"Way back in the year 1872, a forest inspector measured the tree. "It was 435 feet long..." Hayden continued.

"Oooooh!" interrupted the class.

"Even though the top was broken off," Hayden continued.

"Broken off?" asked the class.

"Yes, broken off!" explained Hayden. He was so excited. "So scientists say that the tree was well over **500 feet high**! That's as tall as our Washington Monument!"

"Oooooh!" moaned the class in appreciation, eyes wide open. It was hard to believe.

"And that's not all!" Hayden couldn't wait to share this fact. "The trunk was **18 feet wide**!" Now this was just too hard to believe, as everyone talked at the same time.

"Uh-huh!"

"No way!"

"You *must* be joking!"

Ms. Matson waited for the class to calm down. "That is truly amazing," she said, shaking her head. "Let's try to figure out about how wide the trunk would be," as she walked over to lean against the far wall.

"Now my feet are approximately nine inches long. So if I place each foot about three inches apart (like a ruler), that is approximately a foot. So we should have a pretty good guess at seeing how wide the trunk was." From the wall, she began placing one foot in front of the other, as she and the class counted together: "One, two, three, four..." When they counted to 18, Ms. Matson stopped. She was standing at the built-in cupboards on the opposite side of the classroom. "This is our estimate," she said. The class went wild. It was so hard to believe that a tree trunk could be that big. Many look shocked. Some slapped their heads, while others frowned. Could this be true? Really?

"That's un-be-liev-able!"

"Good golly, Miss Molly!"

"Geez, Louise, how can that be?"

"That tree trunk is almost as wide as our Room 21!"

"So let's see how many of us it would take to give a *circle hug* to that tree," Ms. Matson said. So she asked Hayden to stand where she had started from, and asked Wyatt to stand where she had ended up next to the cupboards. The she found the halfway point in the middle of her 18. Then the class counted nine steps to the right, and had Jillian stand there. Then she went back to the middle, and walked nine steps to the left. And asked Jovie to stand there. So there were four students standing like the hands of a giant clock, at 12 o'clock, 3 o'clock, 6 o'clock, and 9 o'clock. The rest of the class then joined together, holding hands in the huge circle. No one could believe that a tree trunk could be that large! Hayden slowly turned in a circle, pointing to show that the tree trunk would almost fill up the whole classroom. "It's hard to imagine that a tree trunk could be so big," said Ms. Matson, shaking her head. "It would have taken all of us to hug that tree! Now that's what I call a *humongous* tree!"

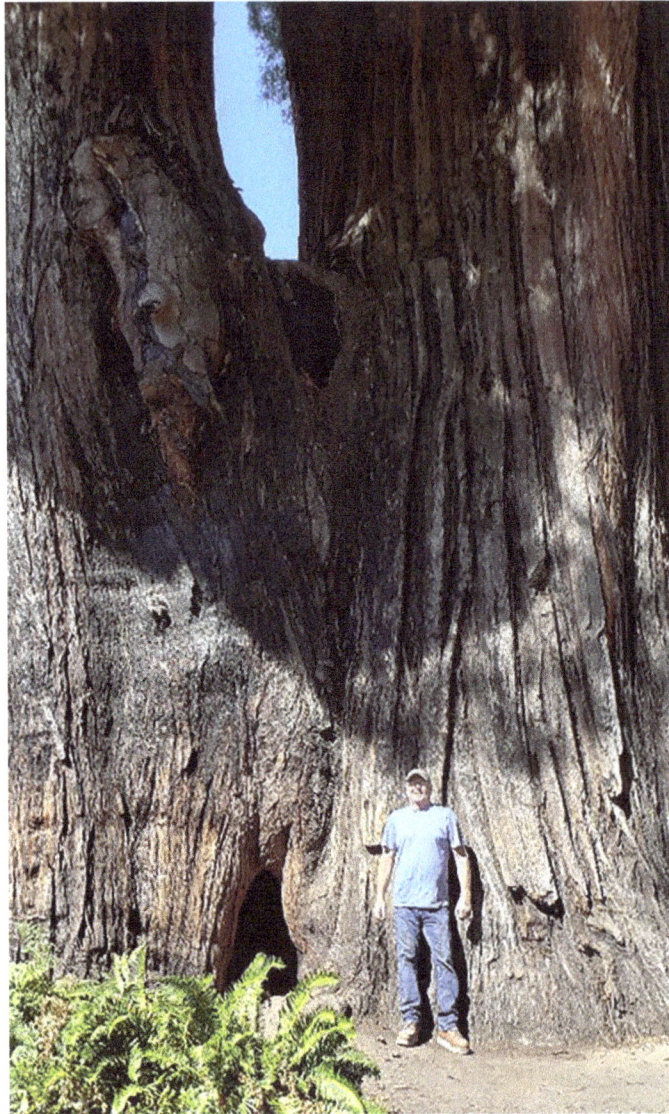

After everyone went back to their seats, Hayden continued. "Since it is so hard to imagine that trees can get so tall, I brought a bunch of pictures to share," Hayden said, as he piled a stack on the table next to the Bonsai tree. "That's a great idea," Ms. Matson said. "We can all look at them in our free time. Thank you for sharing the pictures with us."

The students became quiet, just thinking about it. So Hayden took this opportunity to finish his report. **"Trees are also the *oldest* living things on earth.** They live longer than any other plants or animals. Some trees grow to be 60 to 100 years old, like more and more people. Others live for a 1,000 years. And even some grow to be 4,000 years old, and there are three trees in California that are said to be 5,000 years old.

Can you believe that? And, there is a spruce tree in Sweden that is *9,550* years old!" That sure got everyone's attention.

Hayden bowed. Everyone clapped for Hayden as he sat down. They really liked his project, because he was so enthusiastic, and eager to share what he had learned. Ms. Matson said, "Let's review the two major facts in his project." The class responded that trees are the *oldest* and the *largest* living things in the world today. With smiling bright eyes, the students were thinking that maybe they could learn a lot, after all.

Surprisingly, Hayden jolted up out of his seat like a Pop-Tart, and said, "Hey, wait a minute! Something else I found out, but didn't know how to put it in my report: Did you know that people stop growing taller, but trees keep on growing right up until they die? Trees grow taller, and their trunks grow wider, each year. And did you know that people can lose weight, but trees can't?" Everybody was laughing along with Ms. Matson. It was clear that Haydon enjoyed sharing what he knew.

Chapter 7

TREE ENVIRONMENT

The next day, Wyatt came to the front of the room. He was a fairly new student, and was uncomfortable standing in front of the whole class. He was naturally nervous. The class, of course, knew how he felt, and smiled in encouragement. Wyatt wanted to keep his project short. He wanted to get it over with as quickly as possible. But he had a lot of interesting things to share, so he didn't really know how long it would take. It would probably depend upon how his classmates reacted.

Wyatt set his TREE ENVIRONMENTS poster on the chalkboard tray, as he said, "Different trees grow in different environments, all around the world. No matter where trees live, and how different they look from each another, they all have the same parts: roots, a trunk, branches, twigs, and leaves. Just like humans. No matter where we live, and how different we look from each other, we all have the same body parts: head, neck, shoulders, stomach, arms, hands, legs, and feet."

Wyatt took a huge breath, and said: "Trees cover one third of our world. Trees live in most places, except where it is *extremely* hot or *extremely* cold." He picked up the big world globe out of its frame, and before he could say anything else, the students grinned, calling him *Atlas*. So Wyatt posed like he had big muscles, as everyone laughed. He felt better, sincc thc class was laughing *with* him, not at him. Ms. Matson interrupted, saying, "I am so *impressed* that you all remembered the Greek myth about Atlas!" Turning back to Wyatt, she said, "We learned about Atlas a long, long time ago, Wyatt," she explained. Turning back to the class, she said, "Remember how we thought it was strange that Atlas' punishment was to hold up the sky for all eternity, but all the sculptures and paintings show him holding up the world?" The students all remembered, nodding their heads up and down. A quick discussion followed, about why Zeus had punished Atlas. Then Ms. Matson smiled at Wyatt, and apologized for getting the class off track, and said, "Please carry on, Wyatt. This is so interesting!"

So Wyatt continued, as he pointed to the Arctic. "Way up here at the top of our world is the North Pole, which is actually *in* the Arctic *Ocean!* Although the Arctic Ocean is the smallest of the five oceans, the Artic is land that has been frozen for thousands of miles, by very thick ice. The temperature hardly ever gets above zero degrees, but it is much warmer than Antarctica. There are many wild animals that have adapted to the cold (like the Artic hare, the Arctic fox, wolves, reindeer, moose, the Canada Lynx, Musk oxen, and the Polar bear.) Even though the Polar Bear is called 'the King of the Arctic,' the bad news is that scientists think it will become extinct by 2030." Moans were heard all around the room. "Actually, even though it is so cold there, there are many small plant species (like grasses and mosses) growing there, but no regular-sized trees at all. A few dwarf trees, but that's it."

Wyatt paused and said, "The tops of eight countries are a part of the Arctic Circle, and about four million people live there now, mostly those whose ancestors have lived there for ages and ages. So," he paused again, to make sure that everyone was listening. "What part of America is a part of the Arctic?" he asked. There was a silence for a moment, as everyone was thinking. Then almost everyone shouted at the same time, "Alaska!"

"Correct!" Wyatt shouted back. Everyone was smiling and laughing, while turning in their seats to see Ms. Matson's reaction. Happily, she was laughing, too, holding up two thumbs.

Then Wyatt again pointed to the top of the globe, saying, "This is called the Northern area (remember the North Pole), and its ocean is called the

DR. SHERRY L. MEINBERG

Arctic Ocean. But way down south, here at the bottom of the globe, the ocean is not called the Antarctica Ocean. It is called the Southern Ocean. *How strange is that?"* he asked. Comments were heard around the room.

"Antarctica is made entirely from ice. There is no land. It is also much colder and much windier and much drier than the Arctic. The temperature can get to 90 degrees *below* zero, Fahrenheit! When it snows there, it doesn't melt, making large sheets of ice. The ice sheets have been there for **40,000 years!**" The class reacted to that large number, so Wyatt knew they were all still listening. "The air has no germs or dust, which would be perfect for people with allergies, but the weather is just too cold to live there.

"Antarctica has some interesting features, like a waterfall that runs red, and a volcano that erupts in crystals, but it has no trees, no bushes, and no wild animals. It has no reptiles, no snakes, no cockroaches, and no mosquitoes. It does have one bug (which no one can see, because it is only one centimeter long). It spends nine months of the year frozen solid.
"Like a Popsicle?"
"How can that be?"
"Who could even *see* that bug?"

Wyatt bravely carried on. "Antarctica does have ocean creatures, but most of them are only seasonal visitors. The conditions are just too hard for animals to live there in the winter. The most well-known visitors are krill, seals, porpoises, dolphins, orcas, narwhals, and whales. The visiting birds are the Snowy Owls, the Bald Eagles, albatrosses, and 18 species of penguins. There is also a *giant* sea spider, that is as large as a dinner plate." Wyatt showed the size with his hands.
"Eeuuuw!" was heard all around the room.
"How creepy is that?"
"It gives me the chills just thinking about it!"

"Researchers were recently shocked to discover **77** new unusual species living *under* the ice shelves. But they, too, will be too small to see. So we can expect more discoveries in the future.

"The only people who live in Antarctica are scientists. They use to live in little red huts or cabins, so they could see where their homes were. The weather was so bad, that the scientists sometimes couldn't see anything at all. They were sometimes in a *white-out*, which means that they were in a bad blizzard, and all the landmarks were snow-covered, and nothing could be seen. (It's kind of like when we have heavy fog, and we don't know where we are.) So red paint was used on their cabins, to help them find their way home, so they wouldn't get lost in the storms. They now have a much bigger and better building to live in, altogether.

"Only scientists can live in Antarctica. In order to work there, the scientists have to have had their wisdom teeth and appendix removed. Hopefully, they now have a doctor to live with them. If you want to work there, you have to take a three-week training course first, to see if you can handle the hours and conditions. No tourists should visit Antarctica, because there is nothing to see, and nothing to do, and they would probably freeze to death, because it is so cold there. If you still want to visit anyway, you must send a letter, explaining why it is important to you, and you must wait for a long, long, time to get a return letter, saying why you are accepted, or why not. Know up front that it would be a long time wait, and very expensive."

As Wyatt twirled the globe around, he said, "In the rest of the world, there *are* trees that can live in cold weather, but very few can live up on the highest mountain tops. It's really odd to see what is called a *tree line*, where the forest trees automatically stop, and grow no further up the mountains. They somehow *know* that they couldn't survive in the even colder weather up higher."

Then Wyatt turned around and put the globe in its holder. He picked up four photos and held them in his hands. "Most trees like to grow where it is mild, warm, and sunny year-round. Like all those trees that surround us everyday. So there are many different species of trees living here together. But there are other trees that like dry climates (like deserts). Very few people live in those areas. Trees that live in swamps, jungles, and deserts, look very different from all the other trees, since they live in such tough conditions. They have changed, they have *adapted*, to their environments.

"You already know what Spruce trees look like. They are the ones we all see at Christmas time. They grow in the cold mountain areas," Wyatt said.

"Let me jump in here for a minute, Wyatt" said Ms. Matson. "My brother once owned a Christmas tree farm. It was high on a mountain. His trees were planted in perfect rows, just like stalks of corn or sunflowers. He grew hundreds of Spruce trees. It was a beautiful sight to see." The students were amazed, because they had only seen Spruce trees being sold in Christmas Tree lots, and had never thought about where or how the trees were grown. After the discussion, Ms. Matson said that she was sorry to have interfered with Wyatt's project, and everyone turned their heads to continue listening to his talk about tree environments.

"And you all know what Palm trees look like, because we're surrounded by Palm trees. They like to live where it is very warm or hot. We see plenty of them here in California, or the islands." Everyone agreed.

Then he held up the photo of a Mangrove tree. "The Mangrove is *amazing!* It is the only tree that can live in *saltwater!* Mangrove forests live along the coasts of 118 hot countries. There are up to 110 Mangrove species, from small to large. Their leaves are waxy. Their roots live both under water and *above* the water, since the tides go in and out every day. Both little fish and big sharks like to swim around among their roots."

Wyatt held up the next photo. "There are a few trees that can live in extremely hot environments, like deserts. The United States has four major deserts, as well as some smaller ones. The Mesquite, Joshua, and Yucca trees live in our deserts, along with the Saguaro cactus, which is the desert plant we recognize the most.

The Mesquite tree has a "rough as nails" reputation. It is known as the toughest tree worldwide. They are kind of ugly, being short, and squatty, with few branches. They are covered with sharp, vicious three-inch long thorns. They are known as *Devil trees*. They are considered to be like a *bad weed*, taking over many areas. They are blamed for absorbing so much water that they lower the water table, causing other trees to starve to death. There are 40 Mesquite species worldwide. They are slow growers, at only 2-to-3 inches a year. Yet they can grow up to 20 or 30 feet, over 50 to 60 years. The can live to be 100 years, but the oldest is 1,000 years. They can grow where no other trees can. They grow in the Mojave Desert of California, Nevada, Utah, and Arizona, only around 2,000 to 6,000 feet. The Texas farmers and ranchers hate the Devil trees. But in other parts of the world, these same trees are called "The Tree of Life," by those who see them in a positive way They provide shade and fruit, for birds, animals, and humans. They bloom with yellow flowers, and drop 10-inch long seed pods each fall. The interesting thing about their seed pods is that they can sleep for up to **40 years**, waiting for conditions to be just right for sprouting. *Isn't that amazing?"* Heads nodded in agreement.

Wyatt turned to the class, and said, "No matter how different the trees look, and how different their environments, they all began with a seed, and need sunshine, water, soil, and space to grow."

"Thank you, Wyatt," clapped Ms. Matson, as the class followed. "Very interesting! And who knew you were so *strong*?" she added, as the class giggled. She followed with some review questions, and was satisfied with the class answers.

Chapter 8

TREE ROOTS

Ms. Matson had started a TREE VOCABULARY CHART earlier, and with each tree report, she added special vocabulary words. She started with *seeds*, and added the word *roots*, as it was Jovie's turn to be the teacher. She placed her TREE ROOTS poster on the chalk tray, next to the other posters. Her picture was filled with an underground tangle of roots. And she began.

"Just like *all* green plants, no matter how big and tall they get, each tree grows from a seed. Some seeds are teeny, tiny, and others are lots bigger. The seeds are *all* are different shapes, and colors, depending on their species." Jovie opened up her hand, to show different kind of seeds and nuts.

"The first thing that grows from a seed, is the root. It is the main root, called the *tap root*. It grows straight down into the soil." Jovie pointed to the tap root on her poster. "The underground roots hold the tree steady in the ground. The further down the roots grow, the better they can hold the tree straight. Some tree roots are humongous! The roots of a wild fig in the Echo Caves in South Africa have are 400 feet deep! Can you imagine it?"

"Tree roots grow longer each year. Many tree roots grow for each tree. Closer to the top of the soil, roots spread out like a huge web. Usually, there are twice as many roots below the ground, as there are branches *above* the ground. But many trees actually have *more* roots underground than there are branches overhead," explained Jovie.

"Do you remember our Tree Bridge?" Ms. Matson asked. "Remember how big the roots were, that you had to climb through to get to the trunk of the tree?" Everyone was shaking their heads in agreement. Of course they remembered. "You observed, right then and there, that the roots were even *bigger* than the tree top!" Everyone agreed.

"The tree roots hold the soil in place," Jovie continued. "They keep the soil from washing away in heavy rains and floods. When the soil is held in place, water sinks far underground. It is called the *water table*, which is usually 50 to 100 feet down. But that can change, depending on the time of year. When the snows melt, or rainfall is heavy, or a flood happens, the water table rises. Lot's of water is stored down below.

"Many people need that underground water. They bring it back up by using wells," Hayden added. "Thank you for sharing, Hayden," Jovie smiled, just like Ms. Matson.

Jovie continued. "The main job of roots is to drink up water from the soil. This is important because the water contains minerals that helps the trees grow and stay healthy," she said, pointing at several roots on her chart.

"The tips of the roots—called the *root tips*—are covered with little bitty hairs," she slid her finger over to point out the hairs. "It is these millions of tiny root hairs that collect the water from the soil. They deliver the water up through the trunk to the leaves." She pointed to the trunk of the tree. "The old root hairs die after a while, but new ones keep forming behind the root tips, as they grow."

"Trees usually do things slowly, but they drink water very fast. The big trees can drink over 100 gallons a day. On a warm day, a large shade tree will drink up to as much as 260 gallons of water," Jovie said.

"Oooooh!"

"That sounds like a lot," said many.

"How much would that be?" asked others. Several children shrugged their shoulders at each other. No one knew the answer.

"Let me see if I can answer that for you," Ms. Matson interrupted. "Let me think now. Hmmmm. Can you all see our aquarium?" Everyone turned around to look at the fish tank in the back of the room. It was placed on the counter, next to the sink. Brightly colored fish were happily swimming to and fro. "That large aquarium holds 26 gallons of water. So, a large tree would take ten times that much water. Each day!" The class looked confused. "In other words, Ms. Matson tried again, "It would take ten fish tanks like ours, stacked on top of each other, to hold the same amount of water that one shade tree would drink in one day."

"Oooooh!"

"Awesome!"

"That's amazing!"

"It is also interesting to know that Eucalyptus trees drink more water than any other tree! There are many Eucalyptus trees in Long Beach. And they use so much water that there is a drop in local water table levels. Often, any trees that are planted close to Eucalyptus trees, can't get enough water for themselves. And some get really thirsty, and die.

"As I said before, roots also hold the tree to the ground," continued Jovie. "They anchor the tree in place, holding it up straight. The forests have tap roots in much deeper soil. If trees had no roots, they would all fall over! Or if they don't have enough soil, they will fall over. Most of the trees that people plant on their property, or in our parks, are not planted in deep enough soil. So they don't live as long as they could, and they are much easier to fall in a storm."

"Just like those 500 trees that fell in Long Beach!"

"Just like the trees in our storm!"

"Just like our tree bridge that fell!"

"The wind was way too strong!"

"The rain was way too strong!"

"You got that right!" others added.

Everyone had the same idea. Our city trees were not planted deep enough in the soil, so they didn't have enough roots to hold them. After an exciting discussion, the students thought that plumbing pipes, and electrical pipes, and gas, oil, and steam pipelines (with the active oil fields close by), might have been in the way. Or that the people who planted the trees just didn't know that they should be planted deeper down. After all, the class was just hearing this news, so maybe the planters didn't know about it, either.

"Up to a third of a tree is hidden underground!" Jovie said. "Scientists have observed roots at 20 foot deep, at 33 foot deep, and one at 174 foot deep. "Under proper conditions, most tree roots are 2-to-4 or even 5 times larger than the canopy. And scientists are just now saying that *roots* are the most *important* part of a tree! And that what grows underground is the most *permanent* part of the tree." Jovie bowed, as the class clapped for her project.

"Thank you for telling us about tree roots," Ms. Matson said. "We all learned a lot from you. Thank you for being our teacher for the day!" Jovie blushed as she sat down.

Chapter 9

TREE TRUNKS

Paxton walked to the front of the room, and placed his poster next to the other three. The title said TREE TRUNKS. It showed the trunk of a tree.

"The main tree stem is called the trunk," Paxton began. "It must be very strong, to support the weight of all the tree's branches. The part of the trunk that we see is called the *outer bark*. The outer bark is like our skin. So, I guess you could say that the bark is a tree's skin.

"The outer bark can be as thin as a sheet of paper (as he flapped a paper around), or it can be as much as two feet thick…"

"*Two feet thick?*" the class interrupted.

"Wow!"

"That's *un-be-liev-able!*"

Everyone held their hands apart, trying to gage how thick some tree bark could actually be.

Paxton was glad that everyone was listening. "The outer bark stops the tree from drying out. It has a waterproof coating that covers the bark. It keeps the trunk from losing too much water. The outer bark also keeps the tree from getting too cold, so it is like a great big overcoat. It also protects the tree from the weather, and from any creatures that might want to harm it, like animals, insects, and fungi. The outer bark can even protect some trees from forest fires.

"The young trees have smooth bark. But as the tree grows older, the bark cracks and peels, and some become all wrinkly. And," he paused, *"the tree breathes air through tiny holes in the bark."*

"What?"

"Trees have several ways to breathe?"

"The outer bark is a dead layer, so it cannot grow. So when the tree gets older, and it's trunk gets bigger, the old bark stretches until it cracks or falls off. That's just like when our dead skin flakes off our bodies."

"Like when a snake sheds it's skin," added Hayden.

"Eeuuuuw!"

"The outer bark of each kind of tree has its own pattern of cracks and ridges," Paxton continued. "Each species splits in its own special way. Some are very rough, and some are smooth. Some are papery, and some are really shaggy-looking, some are spotted, and some are dark. One of the ways to recognize different types of trees is by looking at their bark."

"Excuse me, Paxton," said Ms. Matson. "Let me interrupt you with our homework for this evening." Groans could be heard around the room. "Now don't be negative, before you even hear what I have to say," she laughed. "I think you'll like this. We are going to do some bark rubbings."

"Huh?"

"Bark rubbings?"

"What's that?" No one knew what she was talking about.

"Bark rubbings are fun to do," she said, "You will all take some thin newsprint home with you today. Just place the paper on some tree bark, and hold it with one arm across the top. Use your other arm to rub across the paper with the side of a crayon. Try to rub firmly and evenly, in one direction only. A special design will pop upright before your eyes. Just like magic! Then when you are done, draw an arrow to show which is the top of the paper." Ms. Matson demonstrated. "If you don't have any crayons at home, take some home today, with your newsprint."

"Alright!" Everyone liked this idea. What easy homework this was going to be. "You might want to do your bark rubbings from different trees in different colors," she suggested. "It will make the designs easier to see." The class couldn't wait for school to be out, so they could do their homework. "Bring your best rubbings back to school tomorrow, and we'll compare them together," Ms. Matson said. She smiled at Paxton, saying, "Please continue."

"Inside of the tree, next to the outer bark, is a layer of living *inner bark*. And next to the inner bark, is a layer of wood called the *sapwood*. The sapwood takes up the most space in a tree trunk. Sapwood looks totally solid. But it actually has a bunch of tiny hollow tubes running through the wood. It's kind of like our veins.

"The sap from the tree roots—that's the water and minerals taken from the ground—moves up through these tubes to feed the leaves. It is like having tiny elevators, going up!" Everyone giggled at the picture it made in their heads. "Other tubes move the leaf-made food down to feed all the living cells in the trunk and roots. So the sap in *those* little elevators are going down!" It was funny to think of tiny elevators inside of trees.

Paxton continued on. "The center of the tree is called the *heartwood*. It is the hardest and strongest part of the tree. It is like its spine, supporting all the weight of tree.

"Understand that if there is a break in the outer bark, it is just the same as if there was a break in your skin. It would be just as uncomfortable, and would hurt just as much, as whenever it happened to you. *Ouch!*" That startled everyone, and they got the giggles again. Everyone enjoyed hearing about the inside of a tree trunk, and clapped for Paxton.

The next morning, everyone compared their tree rubbings with each other. They found many different textures. All the children agreed that they liked that kind of homework.

Chapter 10

TREE STUMPS & TREE RINGS

As Paxton moved to take his seat, Spencer stepped forward, and placed his poster next to Paxton's poster. It was titled TREE STUMPS, with a picture of a stump.

"I'm sure you have all seen a Tree Stump, either in person or in books." Students were nodding their heads in agreement. "Stumps come about when a tree is cut down, or the trunk breaks off. What is left over is the stump."

"Some trees grow faster than other trees. The slow growing trees usually live the longest, and die of old age. But like other living things, trees may also be killed by accident or by disease, by fires, and by changes in the climate. They can also be killed by being chopped down." Everyone already knew that, nodding in agreement.

"But did you know that some of those stumps are still *alive?*" Spencer asked. Now this was new, the class was thinking.

"*How could they still be alive?*" several asked at once.

"With the whole tree cut off, how could it still even be called a tree?"

"The stump can't make food without leaves, so how can it survive?"

Some students had their arms crossed. Others had frowns on their faces. Others just said, "Un-uh!" nodding their heads back and forth. They just didn't believe it.

"Good questions!" said Spencer. "Stumps can live for *hundreds* of years, without leaves," Spencer continued. "And, like you said, they can't make their own food without leaves. *So, how do they do it?* The trees in the forest are feeding the old stump through their roots! The middle-aged trees in the forest are helping the old stump stay alive! The trees are caring for their own."

The class erupted at the same time: "Really?"

"Just like humans!"

"Just like people!"

"Just like us!"

"One scientist said that he observed a group of surrounding beeches that were pumping sugar to an old stump to keep it alive!" And other scientists have witnessed the same thing.

"Many full-grown trees watch over and take care of the younger trees and the much, much older trees. In the forests, trees of the same species act as a family. They help each other to stay strong. Scientists are now saying that trees have *feelings*.

"Stumps are just like people. Some people have been in accidents, or wars, or have diseases, and parts of their bodies are missing. You all have seen handicapped people with missing arms, or missing legs. And some people can no longer walk, so they use wheelchairs to get around. And other people, because of diseases, must stay in their beds all the time. But they are all still alive, and are called people; they are still called humans. And some tree stumps are still alive, and they are still considered to be trees. They are kept alive by other nearby trees. Those trees are helpful, by sending water and minerals to the stump, through their roots. They want to keep that stump alive. They have known that tree, for many years, and still want its company. Or it might even be the daughter or the mother of the tree close by. *Who knows for sure?*

This demonstration of trees showing caring concern for other trees, was quite shocking to scientists. They realized that they had much, much more to learn about trees.

Spencer then surprised the class by turning over his TREE STUMP poster. This side read TREE RINGS. And he began again!

"Tree Rings tell us about a tree's history. Some scientists say that this is where their *memories* are stored."

"What?"

"Do trees really remember?"

"Well, according to many old fairy tales, the oldest trees are considered to be the smartest, because they have lived so long, and observed so many things. And now, some scientists seem to agree. It's easy to tell the age of a tree, if you come across a tree stump," Spencer said. "Just count the double rings." Everyone already knew that, so they nodded in agreement. No one thought they would learn anything new about the age of a tree.

"Remember when we were studying whales?" Hayden excitedly asked, looking at his friends. "Remember when Ms. Matson told us that we could figure out the age of whales, by counting the rings in their ear wax? *Just like trees*!" Everyone laughed, because Hayden always got so enthusiastic. They remembered that silly discussion from long ago.

This side of Spencer's poster showed a large tree stump with tree rings. He asked Paxton to pass out a paper copy of his Tree Ring poster to everyone. "Now look at the rings," he directed. "The rings are dark and light. The light-colored is for the spring growth, and the dark-color shows the summer growth. You count the two rings together as a pair." He paused. "So, how old is the tree stump that I drew?" he asked. The class counted out loud together. "One, two, three…"

"Twenty-three years!" they shouted.

"You are correct," said Spencer, making everybody laugh.

He sounded just like Ms. Matson. The class looked over at her. She was laughing, too.

"You can also tell something else by looking at the Tree Rings," Spencer continued. "They are not always the same size. And that's because in rainy years, the trees grow a lot, and make thick rings. In dry years, the tree doesn't grow as well, so the rings are thin," he explained. "You can even tell if there was a forest fire the tree lived through, by looking for black rings!"

"Wow!"

"So, can you tell if this tree went through a fire?" he asked the class.

"Yes!" shouted his classmates.

"You are correct!" he said. Everyone laughed again.

"When?" asked Spencer. "How old was the tree when the forest fire happened?"

There was a pause, as everyone counted again.

"Fourteen!"

"When it was fourteen years old!"

"Correct!" smiled Spencer, as everyone clapped. Then he bowed to show that he was through talking, and everyone clapped for his two projects.

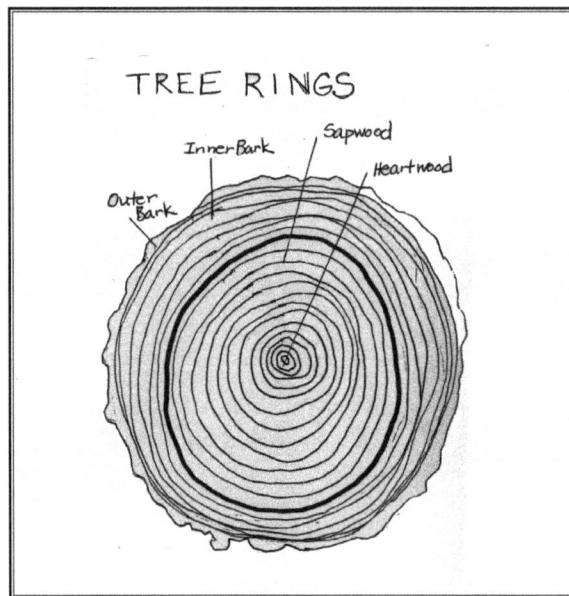

TREE RINGS

Outer Bark
Inner Bark
Sapwood
Heartwood

Chapter 11

LIMBS, BRANCHES, TWIGS & BUDS

Next, Steffi came up to the front of the room. She placed her poster with the others. Her title was longer than the others, and her project was the shortest. It said: LIMBS, BRANCHES, TWIGS, AND BUDS.

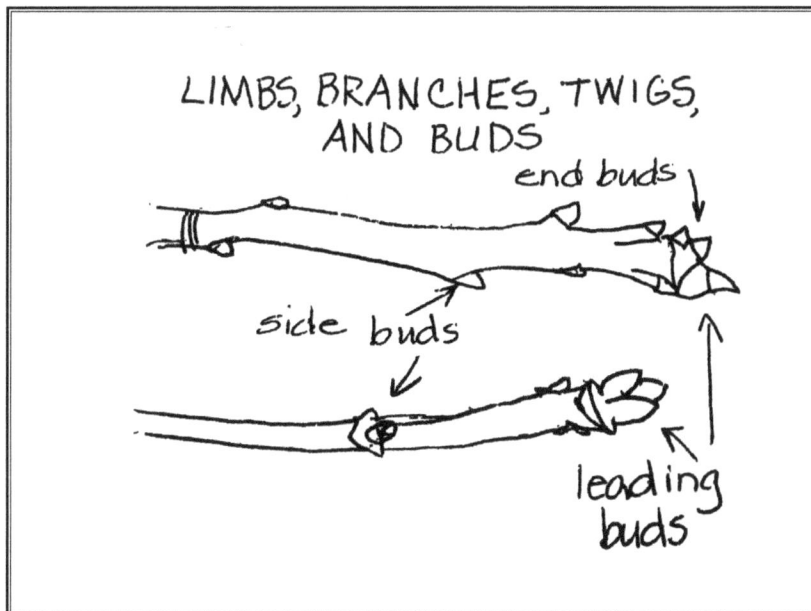

And Steffi began: "The largest parts of the tree growing out of the trunk are called *limbs*. Large *branches* are connected to the limbs. And the parts of the tree growing out of the branches are called *twigs*. Twigs are just very small branches," she explained, as she pointed out the parts on her poster. The limbs, the branches, and the twigs hold the leaves, so that they can get sunlight. But you already know that." Heads nodded up and down all around the room.

"Limbs, branches, and twigs grow longer each year, just like tree roots. Some buds are green, and some are black. Some are large, and some are small. Each tree species has twigs, and buds, that look very different from each other." Steffi passed around some twigs with buds on them, for everyone to see, feel, and compare.

"Notice that there are several buds on a twig. The bud at the tip is called the *leading bud*, or the *end bud*. It grows the most. But if the leading bud is damaged somehow, the next bud down the line will usually become the leader. So then, *it* will grow the most."

"We already heard that shade trees—the ones with the broadleaves—need lots of water. But in the winter, if the ground is frozen, they cannot get water. That's why they shed their leaves, and seal themselves in. When the trees start to seal themselves in, less and less sap goes into the leaves, and the leaves begin to die. That's when they lose their green, and change colors. When the tree is completely sealed in, the leaves fall. It's kind of like the tree is…" began Steffi.
        "… shutting down."
        "… closing up shop."
        "… going on vacation."
        "… going to sleep for the winter."
        Everyone had the idea. They all understood.

"That's right!" Steffi said. "Now when the leaves fall to the ground, they build up into heaps of *leaf litter*. In the forests, they rot and make the soil richer. These leaves provide shelter for beetles, worms, and other tiny creatures. Toadstools also grow in this leafy mixture. So even though the leaves are dead, they are helping the forest."

"At the end of every summer, each tree drops lots of leaves. For instance, one maple tree can drop over a half-a-million leaves. It could make a pile of leaves that is five feet high! That's almost as tall as Ms. Matson!"

"Yow!"

"Cool! Way cool!"

"That's amazing!"

"I'd like to play in a pile of leaves that was *that* deep!"

"Me, too! What fun!" Everyone agreed.

"When the growing season is over, you can see new buds on each twig. These buds are ready for the next year. They contain *all* of the new seasons twigs, leaves, and flowers. These buds remain tightly shut all winter. They are carefully protected from drying out, by being folded up into teeny, tiny packages. Scales, hair, and sticky coats also help to protect them. Then, in the spring, when the sap begins to flow again, the buds grow larger. Then they finally open."

Steffi bowed, and everyone clapped for her. Ms. Matson said, "Class, when you have all had a chance to carefully inspect the twigs that Steffi brought, let's put them together in several wide-necked jars, and place them alongside the windows." She gave three jars to Steffi, as she began to fill them with water. "Hopefully, we can watch the buds burst open. Then we'll be able to see the leaves and flowers unfold and *unfurl*."

"Unfurl?" That was certainly a new word the class was hearing.

Hmmm, let me see if I can explain," Ms. Matson said. "You know the word unfold is opposite of the word fold. It means to open up." Everyone nodded in agreement. Well, the word unfurl and unfold mean pretty much the same thing. Unfurl simply means to spread out. So we will be able to watch the buds open up, and spread out, to let everybody see."

"Unfurl, unfurl, unfurl…" whispered the students, as Ms. Matson wrote the word on the Vocabulary Chart.

Chapter 12

TREE LEAVES

Riley, Maddie, and Emily, came to the front of the room together. They were good friends. Everyone was used to seeing them play together, all the time. And they had seen them do projects together, so everyone expected them to do this project together. They weren't disappointed, as each of girls had a basket full of leaves. Riley placed their poster on the chalkboard tray. It said TREE LEAVES. And she began. "Although there are thousands of species of trees (Remember, Hayden said over 73,000 kinds), they are all divided into just three main groups of *leaves*. They are called the broadleaf, conifer, and palm." She pointed to each picture as she said the name.

"Let's read them together, class," directed Ms. Matson. "That should help us remember the terms." "Broadleaf, conifer, palm. Broadleaf, conifer, palm," the class read aloud together, following Riley's finger. "Good reading," she said. "Please continue, Riley."

"I am going to talk about the broadleaves," Riley explained. "The word *broad* means wide," as she held out her arms. "So broadleaf trees are those that have the wide, flat leaves." She showed examples of several different leaf shapes. "Most broadleaf trees change colors in autumn. Their green leaves turn to yellow, gold, red, orange, and brown. Then the broadleaf trees drop their colorful leaves. Later, they grow new green leaves in the spring." She started handing out examples of broadleaves from her basket. Soon, every desk had several.

"All broadleaf trees have flowers. Seeds are found inside their flowers, or fruit, nuts, pods, or berries. New trees can grow from these seeds."

Riley stepped back, and Maddie stepped forward. "I am going to tell you about *conifers*," she said, pointing to the middle section of the poster. "Conifers mean cones, which is an easy way to remember it. It is a different type of tree. Their leaves look really different from the broadleaf trees," she said, as she showed examples from her basket.

"These kinds of leaves are called *needle leaves*, because they are shaped like skinny needles and pins. Can you see the difference?" she asked. Everyone nodded yes.

"Most conifers are *evergreens*. That means that their leaves stay green all year long. Evergreens grow new leaves before the old ones die. And they only lose a few at a time. So it looks like they *never* lose their leaves. Conifers always look green," she said, passing out examples to each student. Soon her basket was almost empty.

"Conifers got that name because they make their seeds in cones, instead of flowers," she explained. "When a cone dries, it pops open, and scatters the seeds around." Then Maddie stepped backwards, as Emily stepped forward.

"The third group of trees is called palms, or palm trees," as she pointed out the third picture on their poster. "We have lots of palm trees in California." Everyone nodded in agreement. "That's because palm trees grow in warm climates. They are found on islands, and in other hot places."

"Palms either have a very tall, slender trunk, or a short, fat trunk. Instead of branches, most palm trees have a single bunch of feather-shaped leaves. They are called *scale* leaves. The scale leaves can grow as big as **50 feet long.**
"What?"
"*Fifty feet?*" many echoed. Lot's of shaking heads could be seen around the room.
"I never saw palm leaves that big!"
"Me, neither!" others agreed.
"My, oh my," said Ms. Matson. "Let's see how long a scale leaf could grow."
"Oh, boy!"
"Here we go again!" Everyone giggled.

She walked over to the far wall. Ms. Matson began counting, and pacing in a straight line. As the class counted along with her, she walked clear across the classroom, and right out the classroom door. She continued marching in a straight line, clear across the grass, and into the middle of the street. The students were so excited that they jumped out of their seats, and ran to the windows, to see how far she walked. No one could believe it.
"*That's amazing!*"
"*Awesome!*"
"Who would believe that one leaf could be that long?" the children asked each other, as Ms. Matson came back into the classroom.

Emily passed out leaf examples from her basket, to each student. She continued talking. "The best known palm trees grow dates and coconuts. Each tree makes 50 to 100 nuts a year. That's why people like palm trees so much. Dates and coconuts are good to eat. And some people even drink the milk that is inside the coconuts."

All three girls held hands and bowed together. Everyone clapped, as they sat down. "Girls, what a great job you did, gathering all these leaf examples for us!" Ms. Matson praised.

"Riley saved the colorful ones in the fall," both Maddie and Emily excitedly said at the same time.

"And we collected the others in our neighborhoods," said Riley.

"And we didn't have to climb any trees to get them," said Maddie. "The storm knocked them all down!"

"The trees were already dead," Emily explained, "So we didn't kill any of the leaves."

"I'm so glad to hear that you three care about living things," smiled Ms. Matson. "Thank you for going to all that trouble for your project. It is clear that you went out of your way to help us learn."

Ms. Matson turned back to the class. "Now, let's see how much we remember. Let's make a butcher paper chart, and fill it with some of these examples." Everyone was in agreement. This sounded like fun.

Then she got a long, long sheet of butcher paper. With a big black felt pen, she drew three long lines on it. She wrote the name of a tree group at the top of each column. Then she stapled it on the large corkboard, on the long cabinet door, for all to see.

"Now we're ready," she said. Everyone, choose a leaf from the pile on your desk that you especially like." Everyone did. She turned to the three girls. "Would you please pass out some masking tape rolls to each row, please?" Riley, Maddie, and Emily immediately followed the directions.

"Now, as quietly as you can, each of you can stick your leaf in the proper column on our chart," she directed. Then you can go back to your seat, and put tape on your next leaf. We'll have Riley, Maddie, and Emily check to see it you are placing the leaves in the proper columns. Girls, can you do this for us?" she asked. They nodded their heads, eager to check the columns.

"Watch me now, everyone," Ms. Matson said. "See how I can unroll the tape and tear it off? See how I make a little circle of it, with the sticky part on the outside?" Everyone watched, and then made their own. "Please place a little circle of tape on the backside of your leaf." Everyone did. "Some of the bigger leaves might need more tape," she added, seeing that some were having trouble with the larger ones.

All three of the girls felt very important. They watched as each student happily stuck leaves on the chart. It was fun trying to find a leaf that would fit in the remaining open spots. Soon the chart was completely filled with overlapping leaves.

"Wow, class!" Ms. Matson said. "I can't believe how fast you did this! Our whole chart is covered up!" She looked at her helpers. "Now girls, are any of the leaves placed in the wrong columns?"

"No!" said Riley, Maddie, and Emily together, beaming. "They are all correct!" added Emily, as the class laughed.
"Congratulations!" Ms. Matson said. "You are very good teachers. We learned a lot from you!" The girls smiled happily, and they took their seats.

Chapter 13

LEAF SHAPES

"We are still talking about leaves. It is now Jillian's turn to be the teacher," said Ms. Matson, as Jillian walked to the front of the room. She placed her LEAF SHAPES poster next to the other ones on the chalk tray.

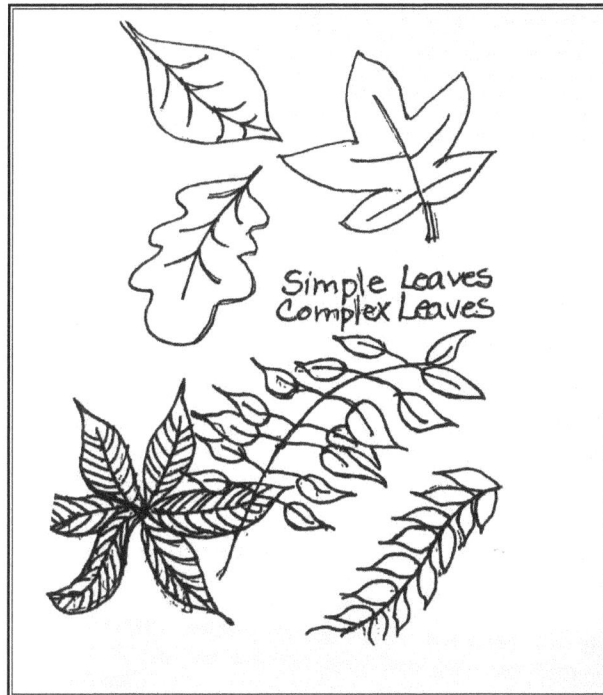

"Some leaves grow all in one piece. These are called *simple leaves,*" as Jillian pointed to her poster. "Simple, simple, simple," softly chanted the class. "Other leaves have several parts," as she moved her finger to show the next group of leaves. "They have separate *leaflets,* all growing from one stem. Leaflets spread out from the main stem, like your fingers spread out." Everyone was wiggling their fingers, as they quietly repeated "Leaflets, leaflets, leaflets. They are called *complex leaves,*" Jillian said. "Complex, complex, complex," the class softly chanted.

"We already know that a tree can breathe through its bark." as she held up one finger, "and it's branches," Jillian said, as she held up two fingers. "But trees can also *breathe* through the veins in their leaves. So they have *three* ways to breathe," as she held up a third finger, "while we have only two ways to breathe," as she lowered one finger. "But because trees are usually much bigger than us, maybe they need that extra breath of fresh air coming in. What do you think?" The students nodded their heads in agreement, saying:

"Could be."

"Sure."

"That makes perfect sense."

"Each leaf is covered by a thin skin. On the underside of the leaf are a bunch of tiny holes, or pores, called *Stomata,*" as she flipped over a leaf. The Stomata are just like the pores in our own skin. They are so little, we can't see them." The class was softly chanting, "Stomata, stomata, stomata…" "By the way," Jillian said, "You will probably *never* hear the word stomata again, unless you become a botanist (who studies life), or an arborist (who is a tree expert who cares for trees and woody plants), or a dendrologist (who studies trees, species, and woody plants in forests). So you really don't need to remember the word stomata, even though stomata is fun to say." The class got a kick out of that, and rolled their eyes while laughing.

"Now we don't have to remember it!"

"Oh, thank you!"

"One less thing to remember!"

"Yes!"

Ms. Matson interrupted, laughing. "I bet you'll remember the term stomata, longer than anything else we learn! Now let's see what else Jillian has to teach us!"

Jillian began as if there had never been a commotion. Holding out the backside of her leaf, she said, "Air enters the leaves through the stomata, and oxygen and water vapor are released." Then she paused. "A tree is constantly inhaling air and exhaling moisture. This outflow of moisture through the stomata of the leaves makes a huge forest area moist and cool on hot summer days," she explained.

"A tree breathes in carbon dioxide (a gas), and breathes out oxygen. We humans do the opposite. We breathe in oxygen and breathe out carbon dioxide. So trees help us, and we help trees, all at the same time."

"Wait a minute, Jillian!" said Stephi wildly waving her arm to get noticed. "I have a question!"

"Okay, let me see if I can answer your question," Jillian said, as the whole class swung their heads back and forth, as if they were watching a tennis match.

"Thank you," Stephi said. "My question is: Since all of our trees lose their leaves in autumn, how do we humans keep breathing?"

"Do any of you think you can answer the question?" asked Jillian.

Some of the girls whispered that Jillian sounded just like a teacher, waiting to see if someone else had the answer first.

Ms. Matson interrupted, saying, "Remember how I said that it takes a lot of courage to be the only one to ask a question? Remember that I said that others may have had the same question, but were afraid to ask it? Let's see who *may* have an answer, before our teacher responds, looking at Jillian. So does anyone here think YOU may have the answer?"

Hayden raised his hand. "I think I have the answer. Our world is hot and cold at different times around the world. So when it is winter for us, it is summer somewhere else. So even though our leaves may have fallen, in other places in the world, their trees have leaves."

DR. SHERRY L. MEINBERG

"Wow! That is such a good answer!" said Jillian. "I would say that you are *correct!*" As the class clapped for Steffi's question, and Hayden's answer, and Ms. Matson waved her imaginary pom-poms around in support.

"Does anyone else have an answer?" Jillian asked, as another hand was raised. "Great. Another brave heart! It seems that Delaney has something to add," as she nodded in her direction. "What is your answer?"
"Remember, when Maddie told us about evergreen trees? Conifers?" she asked. "They are green all year long. So even though the colorful leaves fall and die, there are other trees that keep us breathing!"

"How fantastic! Another wonderful answer! You are *correct*, also!" praised Jillian, as Ms. Matson waved her imaginary pom-poms again.

In an effort to gain back her status as a teacher, Jillian shouted: **"Trees can do what no other human or animal and do!"** Boy that sure got everyone's attention. The class immediately focused on Jillian, who continued: **"Trees make their own food!"**
    "Wow!"
    "I never thought about that before."
    "People can't make their own food..."
    "Animals can't make their own food..."

Jillian continued: "Trees make their own food by using the green coloring in their leaves. None of the green comes from their roots. It all comes from the leaves. This green material is called *chlorophyll. "Let's try saying that word. Chlor-o-phyll.* They chanted the word easily.

"Chlorophyll is one of the most important things in the whole wide world! A tree gets energy from the sunlight. That energy helps the green leaves suck up water and minerals from the roots. The water and minerals mix with carbon dioxide gas taken from the air. The gas and water are somehow mixed into sugar. This sugar is what the tree feeds on. This is called **photosynthesis.** Photosynthesis is a big word that means "putting together with light. This big word sounds hard to pronounce, but let's try it together:" "Photo-syn-the-sis," the class chanted several times, to get it right, as Ms. Matson wrote the words on their Tree Vocabulary Words chart.

"A tree must have the light from the sun to make chlorophyll. Without chlorophyll a plant cannot make food. Have you ever picked up a rock, and saw some grass that grew under it?" Jillian asked. Everyone bobbed their heads up and down. "The grass did not look right. What was wrong with the blades of grass?" she asked.

"They were white."

"They were pale."

"They were not green anymore."

"They looked sick."

"You are all correct! Whatever plant grows in the dark has no chlorophyll. It has no green. Those plants have no light," she explained. "So they would not live very long."

Jillian took a deep breath. "While the leaves make food, the leaves also make oxygen that they don't need. So they get rid of it. They get rid of the oxygen by putting it into the air. Now we already know that the air is made of gasses. One of those gasses is the oxygen that the trees throw away. It is the gas our bodies need. It is the gas that all animals need. It is what we all breathe."

Jillian took a piece of paper out of her pocket, and read aloud from the page, so she would get the facts straight. "Each time we breathe, we take oxygen out of the air. We all breathe a little bit differently, but the estimates are: In one minute you take 12 to 20 breaths:

one minute 12 to 20 breaths

one hour 960 breaths

one day 20,000 to 23,040 breaths

one year 8,409,600 breaths

by age 50 400 million breaths

After the class settled down, Jillian continued. "Even though there are millions of animals, and millions of humans, the supply of oxygen is never used up," as Jillian smiled at them. The reason is that evergreen plants and other green plants keep putting oxygen in the air. When they make their own food, they give off oxygen.

"Without chlorophyll a plant cannot make oxygen. Then both people and animals could not breathe. We are living, and animals are living, because trees are living! Everyone should be a friend to trees!"

"Yes, Jillian," added Ms. Matson. "Trees give us much more than beauty, shade, food, wood, and other things. They give us *life!*" Everyone clapped for Jillian, as she took her seat.

Chapter 14

TREE DIAGRAM

The next report was Jax's turn. Usually, his projects took a lot of time for show and tell. But this time, he wanted to do something a little different. Jax brought up his poster. It only had the title TREE DIAGRAM on it, and nothing else. The class started laughing, and he laughed right along with them, because it was funny peculiar not funny ha-ha.

"I did *not* forget to make my poster," he began. "We are all going to draw a tree diagram together. What I draw on my poster is what you will draw on your paper. Making your own diagram is more fun than just looking at a diagram." He asked Jovie and Jillian to pass out the drawing papers to everyone.

"At first, we are only going to use our pencils. You need to write the title, Tree Diagram, at the top of your paper, like mine," Jax directed. Everyone did.

"Now find the middle of your paper, and draw a line across it, like mine. That will be the ground." Everyone followed the directions, as they giggled. It was funny having Jax as the teacher. "Next, draw the trunk of your tree on the top of the line. Then make a lot of limbs, branches, and twigs." The class enjoyed sketching with their pencils.

"Now let's go underground. We're going to make a bunch of roots, starting with the taproot. Watch me," Jax said. "Remember, the tap root goes straight down." Now write the word, tap root. You can draw an arrow from the label to the picture, if you want to. Now make a lot of roots. Remember, your roots need to be bigger than your treetop. Then write roots somewhere." Jax wrote each word on his chart, as he gave directions. It was easy for the students to follow him.

"Now write root tips. Next, write root hairs, and draw little hairs on your roots. Then write the words, trunk, limbs, branches, and twigs somewhere on your upper diagram. Jax waited while everyone labeled their page. Now add the word canopy."

"What is the tippy top of the tree called?" he asked.

"The crown!" the class called out.

"Correct!" said Jax, with a big smile.

"Just like a queen!" said Laureen. Everyone laughed, remembering when she had worn a crown and pretended to be a queen ant.

"Laureen the queen, Laureen the queen!" the class Chanted.

As the children were finishing their diagrams, Jax continued with his project. "The shape of the crown, and the way the branches grow, are different with each species. Some tree crowns are round and others are spreading kind of flat. Some tree crowns hang down (like Willows), and some slant upwards."

"But sometimes trees are all squished together. There is not enough space between them. They grow so close that they are crowded, and they can't get enough light. Then their natural shape is gone. They must grow tall and skinny, to get some light," he explained. "And sometimes tree shapes are changed by the blasting wind. Their trunks and branches point in the same direction that the wind constantly blows."

Jax paused. "Another reason that the crown might not be its original shape, is that people cut back their trees. They are keeping them from growing too tall. Haven't you seen neighbors trimming their trees?"

Lots of nodding heads could be seen around the room. "Some trees are being pruned so they don't interfere with telephone or power lines, or advertising billboards, or just so the neighbors won't like their trees leaning over the fence onto someone else's property. Also, fruit trees are *pruned* (that means to trim or cut away) to make picking fruit easier."

When everyone had completed that part, Jax continued. "Now, take your green crayon, and draw grass across the middle of your page. Then color in the leaves and fruit in the trees, if you want. Everyone liked this project. It was fun, and everyone made their own diagram. Jax left his finished poster alongside the others on the chalkboard. Everyone worked on their diagrams until the recess bell range. They clapped for Jax's project, as they went out the door.

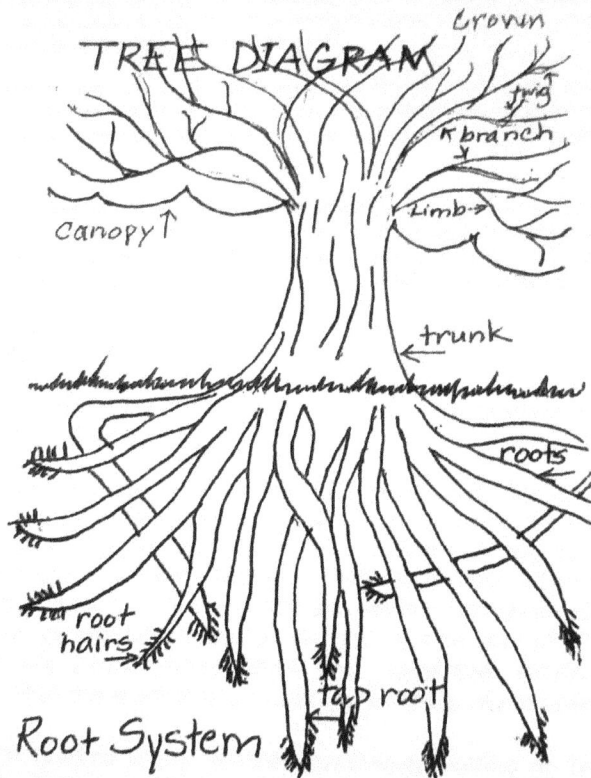

Chapter 15

TREE SENSES

Wensley was the next teacher. Everyone expected something special from him. Wensley always had such interesting things to say. And he often had the most to share. The class was all ears.

"Remember when Jovie said that scientists thought that roots were the most *important* part of a tree?" The class all nodded yes, and they turned around to look at her. "Well, now scientists are saying that trees are very smart!

"Scientists are just now realizing that trees have senses, just like we do. Trees don't have eyes, ears, noses, mouths, or fingers. But they *do* have the senses of seeing, hearing, smelling, tasting, talking, and touching. They can even sense *danger*, so they can defend themselves against enemies."

"Wow!"

"Who knew?"

"That's amazing!"

"This is truly new information!" Ms. Matson said, as the students looked at each other in total surprise.

"And *we* are learning new things about trees, right along with the scientists!" Wensley announced. "They are now telling us that trees experience pain. They say that both trees and plants will "cry out in pain," registering sound in a higher frequency, than we can hear.

When trees are thirsty, they begin to shout and yell and scream (at ultrasonic levels). That's like doggy whistles, that dogs can hear, but people can't. Which is one reason why people should never, ever, carve their initials in trees! That hurts! Then the trunk starts to vibrate, as a way of complaining."

When things quieted down, Wensley continued. Holding up his fingers, while saying, "Scientists also now say that trees have memories, they communicate with each other, they share, and they give help to the sick and weak, when needed. It has even been suggested that trees are displaying *affection* and friendship; that they are very social beings. Think of the stumps that Spencer told us about."

"Double Wow!"

"Just like people!"

"Just like us!"

"In certain species, trees have families. The male and female trees wait for the conditions to be perfect; that there is space enough and light enough for a youngster. Then a seed will be sent to the perfect spot. And the tree parents can watch their child grow close by, and care for it, as needed. When a baby tree is sick, other trees (of the same species) will send it more water and minerals. They care for each other. They connect through their root system. And eventually, the baby tree will be connected to all the trees in the forest, through their vast root system. Their root system is like a giant telephone system. Trees have emotions!

"Now here is something really *amazing*!" Wesley said. "Scientists have long thought that trees had no brains, but they wondered how trees are able to learn, and where trees store what they had learned, and how trees retrieved what they learned. But now, scientists are beginning to think that trees *do* have a brain, and that a tree's brain is in its *roots*."

"Say what?"

"Really?"

"In their roots?"

"Their brains are in their feet?" This was just too much, as laughter was heard all around the room.

77

"I'm not kidding!" Wensley said forcefully. "Trees are similar to octopuses. Octopuses have nine brains. Each of their eight arms has a mini-brain at its tip, with a larger central brain—for overall control—in their heads. For this reason alone, some scientists say that octopuses are considered even smarter than dolphins (which have even bigger brains that humans!). Other scientists simply say that *both* are the smartest sea creatures in the ocean. They are not willing to say that either one is smarter than the other.

"Anyway, the brains in their roots continue to grow, as the trees grow. As a tree root comes upon any toxic substances, large rocks, or unfit soil, it analyzes the problem, and makes adjustments. The root tip then either changes directions, or moves over, under, around or through the problem. The roots take action slowly, but it works for them. So they can think for themselves.

"Trees connect with other trees through their root systems. And they can even recognize their own roots, and their family's roots, as well as members of the same species, on the other side of the forest. They even recognize the roots of other tree species, but they can't communicate with them. And the trees know who their enemies are.

"Trees stay connected, and communicate, in several ways. They communicate through the Wood Wide Web (which is like a forest Internet or cell phone). They also communicate through electrical and chemical signals, their sense of smell, taste, gases, and even sound waves. Some scientists have recorded crackling roots, saying that other trees reacted to it, and "*heard* it."

"And other scientists have said when trees of a species live together in a community, they work together, so they are all equally successful. Their nutrients and water can be divided equally between them, so that each tree can grow up to be the best it can be."

"Among trees, each species may fight other species for space. Beech trees harass other species, especially oaks. They take over every inch of space that the oak tree is not using. Then it tunnels beneath the oak, stealing its water and nutrients. And it grows its own crown up over the top of the oak crown, stealing its sunlight. The distressed tree will put up a fight. But, eventually, the oak weakens, and slowly starves.

"That's not right!"

"Ooooh!"

"How sad."

"If another species tries to gain more space for themselves, by crowding out the other species, there may be a war. There will be a fight for light, or a fight for water, or a fight for both. Their long, slim, branches act like whips in the wind, lashing out in all directions, which might damage the crowns of closer trees. But the fight would be in slow-motion, over a long period of time.

"Usually, if a loner tree is involved, no one will bother it, unless it starts causing a grab for space. Trees can't communicate with other species, as they all have different languages."

"Again, just like us!"

"Most of us don't know other languages!"

"Most of us only know English!"

"If trees are attacked, they aren't afraid to fight back, as the following examples show," Wensley said. "Trees *feel* when they are bitten. When something bites it, the tree knows just what to do. The tree can *taste* who is nibbling. Whenever a bug or an animal bites into its bark, or a branch, or a leaf, it leaves a bit of saliva in the wound...."

"Eeuuuw!"

"Gross!"

"Icky!"

"Wait up guys!" Wensley said. "Wait for the good part! Every animal's spit leaves a different *taste*. As soon as the tree figures out which animal it is dealing with, the tree begins to pump a liquid into the bite site. It tastes really, really bad, and sometimes it's poisonous. And the biters quickly move on.

"When Bark Beetles attack, the trees release a *sticky*, icky, bitter something called pitch. And the Bark Beetles get stuck. Then the trees inform the other trees, by using a special *scent*. So the other trees *smell* the message, and immediately start producing pitch, before the Bark Beetles get to them. Isn't that amazing, that trees can *warn* each other?

"When aphids or other insects eat an oak's leaves, the tree sends out an *electrical* signal to warn the neighboring oaks. When those trees hear the distress signal, they pump up a bitter-tasting *chemical* into their leaves, to get rid of the insects.

"Another example comes from Africa, where trees can warn each other. Giraffes love to eat the leaves of the acacia trees. You've all seen pictures of tall giraffes eating the crowns of acacia trees. The acacia trees don't like this, of course. So they have long sharp thorns to keep all animals from eating them. But the giraffes have the longest tongue, and the toughest mouth, so they can eat their favorite food anyway. So when the tree figures out that a giraffe is munching on its leaves, it begins to pump poison into its leaves, and shoots out ethylene *gas* to 300 feet to warn the neighboring trees, to get ready, because here they come!

"One last example," said Wensley, "because it's so hard to believe! It's not a pretty picture, but it's *true*." Get ready! Okay. Here goes: Some trees can call on animals to help them. For instance, the elm tree knows when caterpillars start nibbling their leaves. So they call on the enemies of caterpillars, which happen to be *wasps*. The wasps smell the chemical message, and instantly respond. So the wasps come flying in and lay their eggs *inside* the dead bodies of the caterpillars. When the eggs hatch, they eat the caterpillars from inside out!"

"Eeuuuuuw!"

"Gross!"

"Icky!"

"Why did you tell us that?" some complained.

"Now I'll have nightmares!" screeched a girl.

After the noise settled down, Wensley said, "Moving on. I just have one last thing to say. Even severely damaged trees with major branches broken off, can grow replacement crowns."

"Excuse me, Wensley," said Ms. Matson. "Let me interrupt you for a minute, with my own example. Years ago, on the 4th of July night, my house caught fire, from a bottle rocket, shot from the next block. The garage, the house roof, and almost everything we owned—furniture, paintings, and clothes—burned up in the fire. Everything was gone. The next morning, my husband had to go to the store to buy a broom and dust pan, so we could start cleaning up. Our beautiful Apricot tree was burned completely black. It was horrible looking, like a scary Halloween picture. But since we were focusing on everything else, thereafter, we never got around to chopping down the tree. We never even looked in the backyard anymore. It was in such bad shape. After a couple of years—SURPRISE!—the tree had regenerated itself, and was all green, and beautiful once again. So trees can take a great deal of punishment, and overcome their health issues, to become healthy again, with time. Our beautiful tree even started growing apricots again, and the whole block was happy, because every year, my son made apricot jam, which he shared with the neighbors." The students had plenty of questions, which Ms. Matson happily answered. Then she apologized again for getting the students off track, and turned back to Wensley.

Wensley ended his project by saying: "The slower the growth, when the tree is young, the more it is expected to live to an old age." The class loudly applauded his presentation, having learned so many new and unusual facts about trees, in such a short time. Wow! Each student had a lot of friends and family members to share what they had learned today.

Chapter 16

DO TREES SLEEP? DREAM? COUNT?

As Delaney walked to the front of the room, everyone knew that her project would be short, short, short, because she didn't like standing alone in front of the class. But she always had something interesting to share. When Delaney placed her poster on the chalk tray, everyone giggled and laughed, rolling their eyes at each other. She pointed to her poster and read, "Do trees sleep? Do they dream? Can they count?" She looked at the class, and said, "These questions were hardly ever asked by anyone, because it seemed like they were such silly questions. But, these questions were on our class list of "Things We'd Like to Know." So I thought I'd check out what scientists think about these questions.

"And *now*," she continued, "scientists are telling us that, yes, indeed, trees *do* sleep at night! They were surprised to find that trees sleep, but they still don't know if they dream, or not. So they are trying to find out." This was hard to believe, for many.

Delaney continued. "It is now said that trees that live in extremely cold weather, *hibernate*, just like bears. They look like they are dead. When trees awaken from their deep winter sleep, it is a slow, slow process, taking many days. Warm temperatures and a longer day length wake up many trees. Some trees wait until it is light for 13 days *in a row* before they fully wake up. So scientists are saying that trees have a way to count. Then they know that it is really spring. Apple trees count the number of warm days that reach 68 degrees Fahrenheit. It appears that all species have a different time and a different way to awaken. That's because if they wake up too soon, and *unfurl* too early, a late frost could freeze them. Some scientists even say that the younger trees are awakened by their mothers, just like humans.

"Scientists in Finland, Austria, and Hungary, recorded the night cycles of trees, and were surprised to see that when trees were measured an hour after sunset, their branches relaxed; they dangled down a little; they drooped." (Delaney hung her head, shoulders, and arms down, to demonstrate, as everyone giggled.). "Then, when it starts getting light in the morning, the trees begin to perk up again. (Delaney perked up, as everyone laughed.) "It takes about three hours to get back to their normal position, in the morning. It takes an average of 30 minutes for human brains to fully awaken and recharge. Now why do you think that is so?" Delaney asked, giving the class a questioning glance. A few squirmed in their seats, as others shrugged. They didn't want to use their brains. They wanted someone else to give them the answer.

"Why does it take so much longer for trees to wake up?" After a lively discussion, some of the students finally decided that trees are so much bigger than humans, that they need more time to wake up. Other students thought that the trees have many, many more brains that need to wake up. A few others said that both ideas worked together.

"Wow!" said Delaney. "Look at us! We're acting like those scientists that fight over different opinions, that haven't been proven yet. Well, it's something to think about," she said, as she moved on, continuing with her project.

"At night, the trees don't make oxygen, but in the morning, the leaves start to make sugar again, so more oxygen is made. So the trees take a break at night, just like humans! Just like all of us!" she gestured.

"But if trees aren't getting enough sleep, it affects the trees in much the same way as humans: it is life threatening. In some towns, and especially large cities, there are many outdoor lights, flood lights, street lamps, and business lights that stay on all night long. And for good reasons: as a safety measure, as well as to discourage prowlers, burglars, and violence. But this causes problems for local trees, because they need to rest at night. Scientists think that by not giving these trees total darkness each night, they are limiting their lives; that they can't grow to be as old as they could be. Scientists are looking for some kind of compromise. Maybe something like motion lights in certain areas. *Who knows?* But it is interesting to think about.

"Some tourist cities, like Las Vegas, keep strong, bright lights on all night long. The lights are so bright at night in Las Vegas, that they can be seen 90 miles away! And the bright lights make it difficult to see the stars at night. Luckily, Las Vegas is a desert town, and few wild trees are growing there."

Everyone clapped for Delaney. Her project was short, but they all learned something exciting to share with their friends and family.

Ms. Matson said, "Class, since Delaney brought up the "Things We'd Like to Know About Trees" chart, this would be a good time to discuss what we now know, and what hasn't been mentioned, so far. They reviewed the questions, and found that they had learned most of the answers. They discussed the three questions that had not been touched upon.

(7) **"Do trees sweat?"** Ms. Matson nodded her head up and down, as she explained that, "Sometimes trees can get way too hot, and just like humans, they sweat. Researchers have learned that trees continuously sweat water through their leaves, when they are experiencing extreme heat."

(5 & 9) **What makes trees get sick?** and **Do trees ever get afraid?** Know that sick trees will recover, if they get enough help from other trees (which is not good news for loner trees). Even battling a disease, they can live a very long life." Ms. Matson added: "A healthy tree's life can change at any time, for a number of reasons. There are many ways

in which trees might get sick, such as lacking water or lacking minerals. Oddly enough, other plants can be an enemy, such as ivy, honeysuckle, and mistletoe. They are like boa constrictors, strangling their victim. (Although mosses don't damage trees.) You already know that a ton of insects are a constant bother to trees. Trees get sick because of insects, like mites, aphids, and even caterpillars that damage their leaves. Pests can cause trees to lose their bark. Large animals, like deer, bear, and humans, damage their bark. Carving initials or scratching anything into the bark of a tree can cause severe problems. Excessive or clumsy pruning can cause problems. Environmental changes, like water shortage, or floods, heat waves, fire storms, poor soil, landsides, and excessive wind can cause health problems. And, of course, there are accidents, fungi, viruses and bacteria.

"And if all that weren't enough," Ms. Matson said, "dogs can cause trees pain. You have all seen dogs mark any areas they consider theirs. They are marking their territory. It is a way for them to send a message to other dogs, saying, "Hey, I am here!" or "This is my spot!" or "This tree is mine!" But dog urine can disfigure trees, giving them a mangy-looking bark that easily peels off. Check out the lower two feet of a tree trunk," she suggested, "and see if there are any long, thin, cracks or splits in the bark. If so, you'll know that dogs have repeatedly urinated on the tree. The chemicals in dog urine can soak through the outer bark, leaving the tree open to harmful diseases and pests, damaging the inside of the tree. And the dog's urine can also seep into the soil, causing toxic levels and tree dehydration. (Dehydration means the loss of water). And dog urine can kill the roots affecting water and nutrient absorption, which kill the roots, causing severe damage to the tree." The class was shocked. *Who knew?* Several students had dogs for pets, and this was something they never even thought about. The whole class discussed ways in which dog owners could help the trees. They couldn't wait to get home to tell their families, what they had learned today. Shocking!

Ms. Matson ended with, "Scientists say that the constant stresses on trees are so great that most will die much earlier than expected."
    "Oh, NO!"

"I wish I didn't know that!"

"People are walking their dogs all the time, and don't even know that they are hurting the trees!"

"Maybe by the time we're adults, people will take better care of our trees.

Chapter 17

FINAL REPORTS

During the following week, the last projects were shared with the class, adding a few more interesting tree facts:

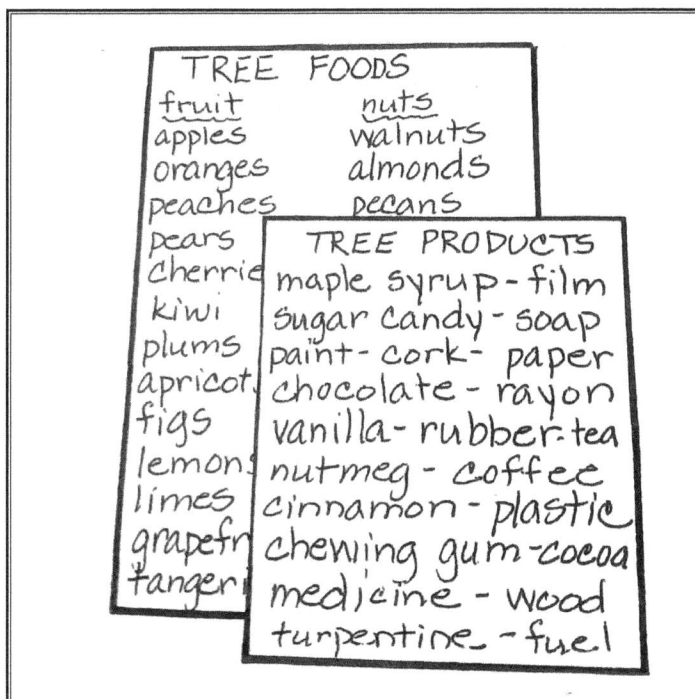

TREE FOODS

fruit	nuts
apples	walnuts
oranges	almonds
peaches	pecans
pears	
cherrie	
kiwi	
plums	
apricot	
figs	
lemon	
limes	
grapefr	
tanger	

TREE PRODUCTS

maple syrup - film
sugar candy - soap
paint - cork - paper
chocolate - rayon
vanilla - rubber - tea
nutmeg - coffee
cinnamon - plastic
chewing gum - cocoa
medicine - wood
turpentine - fuel

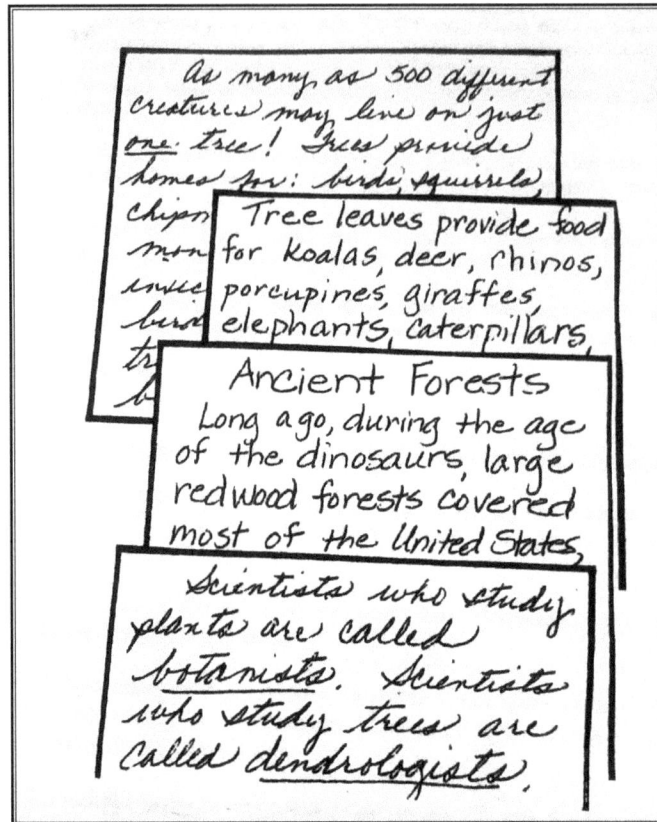

As many as 500 different creatures may live on just one tree! Trees provide homes for: birds, squirrels, chipmunks, mice, ...

Tree leaves provide food for koalas, deer, rhinos, porcupines, giraffes, elephants, caterpillars,

Ancient Forests
Long ago, during the age of the dinosaurs, large redwood forests covered most of the United States,

Scientists who study plants are called botanists. Scientists who study trees are called dendrologists.

1. Scientists have discovered that the more you talk to your trees (either indoors or outdoors), or play music, you are helping them to grow.

2. Trees especially respond to jazz and classical music.

3. Potted trees respond to your voice.

4. Your Indoor plants and potted trees will miss you, when you are not around. While you are on vacation, or in your house for a long period of time (recovering from broken bones or just staying in your house, or such), when you go back to school or work, your indoor potted trees will miss you, because they have no underground connections through their roots.

5. Some scientists have even said that indoor potted trees may even be jealous, if you spend more time with other trees. They want equal time.

6. Trees don't have a heart, but they do have a pulse—a slow heartbeat. Yet the inner part of a tree trunk, is called the heartwood.

7. Every tree in the forest is valuable to the community, and worth keeping alive as long as possible (which is why they keep stumps alive).

8. Trees in a forest like to bloom at the same time, so that the genes of many individual trees can be well mixed.

9. Conifers send their seeds out into the world at least once a year.

10. Before they bloom, shade trees agree among themselves, as to when they should send out their seeds. Should they go for it this coming spring? Or wait another year, or two?

11. The air in forests is almost germ free. Somehow, trees are able to disinfect their surroundings.

12. New trees that grow close to shade trees have a short life, because they live mostly in the shadows. They need light, and don't get enough. So many die at an early age.

13. Just like humans must pay their phone bill, the fungi demand up to a third of the tree's food and minerals for the use of the Wide Wood Web (the forest internet). Sounds like trees pay more for their services, than humans do.

14. A pair of trees of the same species, are careful not to grow thick branches in each other's direction, sharing light and space. But they *do* grow shoving branches toward other species.

Chapter 18

EASTER ISLAND CATASTROPHE

"Today is the last day of our Tree projects," said Ms. Matson. "You all did such a great job with your projects. You all know, it is so *important* for us to take care of our trees. We now have laws to protect our trees, here in America. But the trees are still in *trouble, worldwide.* People are chopping them down faster than we can regrow them. And many other countries don't have laws to protect their trees. So I am going to do my own Tree Project, by telling you a *true* story."

The class was surprised, looking around at each other. *What was going on?* They watched as Ms. Matson placed her poster on the chalk tray, just like everyone else had done. The title of her poster was EASTER ISLAND, which showed a beautiful island.

And Ms. Matson began: "This island was named Easter Island, because a Dutch explorer *re*discovered it on Easter Sunday, in the year 1722 (300 years ago). It is said to be the loneliest island in the world, because it was so far away from any land. It was almost 3,000 miles from South America, surrounded by about a million square miles of the Pacific Ocean." Ms. Matson showed where the island is located, on the pull down map of the world.

"I know you have all heard of this island before…," she began, when she was quickly interrupted.

"Say, what?"

"Uh-uh," many shook their heads back and forth.

"No way!" some of the boys shouted, as they crossed their arms over their chests, and scowled.

"What are you *talking* about?"

"But you *do* know,"Ms. Matson insisted, as she turned her poster around, that showed huge statue heads.

"Oh, *that* island."

"Sure!"

"Of course!"

"Yes!"

"I remember now!"

"This island is *famous!*"

Such responses were heard all around the room. Everyone knew a little *something* about the island. "It is said that the statues were carved to honor their ancestors, but no one *really* knows the answer." More comments were made, before she could start again. The students were so excited.

91

Ms. Matson smiled at everyone. "You *do* remember! It is the island that is famous for having many *gigantic* stone statues on it. They were carved hundreds of years ago," she reminded them. "When I was much younger, and became interested in Easter Island, it was thought that there were 60 statues, which I thought was unbelievable! In later years, the number rose to 200, then 300, then 600! Lately the count has grown to 900, and now they are saying nearly *1,000 statues* are on the island. Wow! As the years go by, scientists keep finding more and more statues.

"The island is small. Its longest side is 15 miles, and it is only 11 miles across at it's widest point. It had been formed by three volcanoes." Everyone remembered when they had studied about how volcanoes formed islands. That had been really interesting to learn about.

"Let me tell you something very interesting about this island. Scientists used to *argue* about who had once lived on Easter Island. Some said that a group of people who came from the west lived there. Others said that a group of people who came from the east lived there. There was evidence for both opinions. Scientists argued about it for many years. After much research and digging and learning, it turned out that both groups were right!" The class giggled. They pictured in their minds a bunch of mad scientists arguing over their beliefs.

The story finally became clear. Around 400 A.D., the first group found it's way to the island. This group was from the *east*. They were Incas from Peru. They had been the *losers* in a war in Peru, and had to leave. They moved to this island, and brought many things with them. They brought things like sweet potatoes, plants, and other food to grow. They brought chickens (and stowaway rats, which caused a problem many years later.) They brought their culture, language, music, and their beliefs, and their religion. These people were called the Long-ears."

"Long-ears?"

"What a funny name."

"Why were they called the Long-ears?"

THE TREE BRIDGE

"So glad you asked," Ms. Matson said, as she wiggled her eyebrows at the group. "They were called the Long-ears because they pierced their ears. They wore large round plugs in them, instead of dangling earrings."

"Eeuuuuw!"

"Ouch!"

"Now you've seen pierced ears before," said Ms. Matson. "Lots of people wear pierced earrings." Everybody nodded in agreement. Several pointed out the two girls in class, who were wearing them.

"Well, this group of people wore round plugs that were really heavy. It was the sign of the ruling class, where they had come from. They started out sticking little reeds in their earlobes. Then, over time, they kept adding more reeds, until they stretched the holes big enough to, put seashell plugs in their ears. These plugs were so heavy, their earlobes stretched in length. Because this was so unnatural, this group of people were called the Long-ears."

"Many years later, a second group of people arrived on the island. They came from one of the Polynesian islands from the west. They were called the Short-ears, because their ears were normal. The Short-ears were made to work for the Long-ears. They were slaves for 200 years. They were slaves for so long that they forgot their own culture and traditions and religion.

"The Short-ears did not like being slaves. So the Short-ears finally rebelled. They started fighting the Long-ears. The Short-ears won the war, and killed *all* of the Long-ears. They were still so angry that they knocked over most of the largest statues. And they broke the necks of many statues. They removed the eyes of all the statues. Then the Short-ears ruled the land."

"Ooooh!"

"Anyway," Ms. Matson said, "the most important thing to remember is that, at first, the island was *beautiful*. It had all of the trees, plants, animals, birds, and insects that most islands have. It seemed to be perfect,

93

so the Short-ears decided to stay there." The students took some time to discuss beautiful islands they had seen on television or in the movies.

"But…," Ms. Matson started.

"Uh-oh!" many students said. They didn't like the sound of this.

"Oh, no!"

"Something went wrong!"

"I don't want to know," some said, as they covered their ears.

"But," Ms. Matson continued. "None of the people knew about trees. They didn't know that they should *re*plant trees. They thought (just like everyone else in the world at that time), that there were so many trees, and the trees had lived so long, that the trees would last forever." The class was silent, hanging on every word.

"As the years went by, more and more babies were born on the island. And more and more rats were born, too, at a much higher birthrate. (A single mating pair of rats reproduce 6-to-18 pups, every six or seven *weeks* (which became a major problem, as rats had no predators.) Within one year, *one* mother rat could have around 1500 pups. When you consider that the peak number of humans on the island was 17,500 versus the same peak number period with 1.6 million rats, you can see the problem. The rats ate almost anything, and they *loved* seeds. So no seeds were left, even if people were able to grow more trees.

"But farming wouldn't work anyway, because of the strong winds and salty spray. (Salt will kill most plants.) So no one could grow anything. So more and more trees were chopped down, and the land was used for housing and streets. Everyone used even more trees for making houses, large sailing boats, personal canoes, and decorations. They ate the food that grew on trees. They also ate many of the animals that lived in the trees. They used even more trees for fires to burn their dead. They also used wooden tablets, to record their language (since they didn't have paper). So, the trees were used for everything!"

Ms. Matson paused to be dramatic. "After many, many generations, someone cut down the very last tree."

"Ooooh!"

"OH, NO!"

"Their food was all gone (no more bananas, coconuts, or figs), so the people ate all the chickens, and then started eating the *rats,* which was the only animal left. Then, when the rats were all gone, some scientists suggest that the people began to eat other humans."

"Ooooh!"

"Gross!"

"Ick!"

"How could they *do* that?"

The students were upset, in more ways than one. It took a little time for the class to settle down. Ms. Matson showed a picture of Easter Island, as it looks now. The picture showed a hilly, bare island. "There is no beauty there now. There is no cooling shade. The forest is gone; the soil is gone; the wild animals, insects, and birds are gone. There is nothing left but mostly black, rocky ground. There are no streams (fresh water comes from wells, and the crater lakes).

"Their paradise was ruined! Their paradise was ruined because there were no more trees or bushes, animals, or birds, so their way of life completely changed. Forever."

"Ooooooh!'

"What a story!"

"That's so sad!"

"It makes me want to cry!"

"Too bad the story really happened!"

"Yes,"said Ms. Matson. "Easter Island is a perfect example of how trees, plants, insects, animal, birds, and people, are *interdependent.* We are all in a Web of Life together. We are all connected. We are all interrelated, in one way or another. We need each other," she said, as she put her hands together, joined, and intertwined the fingers of both hands. The students copied her, and placed their fingers together, also. Ms. Matson bowed like many of the speakers had done. The class giggled and laughed that she was copying the students, like the students copied her. They clapped long and hard.

Later in the day, during the last hour of class, Ms. Matson said, "As I recall, you didn't think that there was much more to learn about trees. Do you remember that?"

"Yes!" roared the class.

"Did you all learn something new about trees?" Ms. Matson asked.

"Yes!" roared the class.

"Right on!" Ms. Matson said. "Just look at all the new words you learned," as she showed the class the TREE VOCABULARY chart. "A few of the words you already knew, but many of the words were new to you, and now you know the *meaning* of all those words. Give yourself a hand," as they all clapped and celebrated their growing knowledge.

TREE VOCABULARY

Seed	cone	pod
seedling	bark	crown
broadleaf/broadleaves	inner bark	simple leaf
conifer	outer bark	complex leaf
palm	sapwood	leaflet
evergreen	sap	veins
needle leaves	heartwood	stomata
tree line/timberline	limb	oxygen
root	branch	chlorophyll
tap root	twig	photosynthesis
system	leaves	soft wood
root hairs	bud	hard wood
trunk	leading bud/end bud	species
tree rings	unfurl	fungus/fungi
black ring	Wood Wide Web	stump
botanist	Mesquite Tree	leaf litter
dendrologist	Antarctica	Easter Island
Mangrove Tree	clear cut	pioneer trees
Artic	canopy	prune/pruned
water table	Eucalyptus Tree	root tips
Spruce Tree	Palm Tree	Devil Tree
interdependent	The Tree of Life	root tips
dehydration	absorb/absorption	arborist

EPILOGUE 19

TREE FRIENDS FOREVER

As it is with all classes, over time, the students became interested in other subjects. They became excited about new learning. Although they studied about many different things, they never forgot about what they had learned about trees.

The students in Room 21 began a lifelong friendship with trees. They decided to save trees at school *and* at home. They shared what they learned with other classrooms, their families, their friends, and neighbors. They became good examples of the old saying, "It's what you *do* with what you know that counts!"

At school, they tried not to waste paper. And, they used both sides of their papers. They even used the backsides of graded papers for writing rough drafts, and for scratch paper. After artwork or accidents, the students cleaned up after themselves with rags or sponges. They didn't use paper towels anymore.

At home, the children encouraged their families to cut down on the use of paper products. When shopping, they would take their own paper bags for reuse. Others would take net or canvas bags with them. Sometimes, if an item was small, they would put it in their pocket or purse (with the receipt), and say, "No thank you. I don't need a bag. I want to save a tree!"

Then the students learned that the old newspapers would be shredded, mashed, washed, and made into paper again. Because this would save even more trees, Room 21 began a recycling project. They collected used newspapers from their neighbors every week. They brought the papers to school, and stored them. When they had enough, the newspapers were taken to a local Recycling Center.

The children were surprised to find that they received money from the Recycling Center for all the used paper. They thought they were just doing a good deed for the earth. The class voted on what to do with the money. It was decided that, because so many trees had been lost during the storm, that Room 21 would buy a tree. The students wanted to plant it in Goldenrod Park. We informed Goldenrod Park supervisors that they could choose a tree that would fit well in their park, and that the class would pay for it.

When the people in the City Park Services heard about our third grade class project, they were excited. So the Goldenrod Park officials decided to have a big picnic for Room 21. Everyone who had ever used the park were invited to come. Friends, neighbors, and whole families came to the picnic. Lots of little brothers and sisters, and babies in strollers, came. Everyone brought their own lunches. The school cafeteria provided 32 lunch bags, one for each student in Room 21. Goldenrod Park workers served punch and cookies to everyone. Many speeches were made by adult officials, saying how proud they were of the students, and what a good job Room 21 had done.

When the large sapling was lowered into the hole (that had been conveniently dug by the park workers the day before), each of the students in Room 21 got to place a big shovel full of dirt into the hole. Then the park officials gave a giant vitamin pill to Ms. Matson (that was almost as big as her hand), to throw into the hole. Which she did. And then the workers filled up the hole again. Everyone whooped, clapped, and some even whistled. Photographers took pictures for the newspapers and newsletters. Parents took photos for their family scrapbooks. It was a great day!

For years thereafter, former students would come back to Room 21, to visit with Ms. Matson, and to give a report about "their" park tree. Everyone loved to watch the tree grow.

About the Author

"Books are my life!" says Dr. Sherry L. Meinberg. "I read books, I write books, I edit books, I donate books. I eat, sleep, and breathe books."

When she retired from teaching in public schools (after 34 years), Dr. Meinberg owned over 6,000 children's books, which is why she also became the school librarian. She generally reads a book a day, unless she is writing. She is a true bookworm. A large mishmash of books are stacked in every room in her house, even though she has one room as a dedicated library. She regularly donates books to libraries, schools, shelters, and individuals. Even her car license says READ4ME, and its license plate holder says SO MANY BOOKS, SO LITTLE TIME. On several occasions over the years, when she returned to her car after shopping, she came across a small crowd of people, who were looking at her license plate. They had taken bets as to whether she was a teacher, a librarian, a professor, or an author. And she happily said that they were all correct! Dr. Meinberg absolutely loves storytelling, and has carried on a lifelong affair with the printed word. Books are a source of joy for her, as she edits manuscripts by new authors of all ages. She is a true bibliophile. Dr. Meinberg later became a core adjunct professor, and supervisor of student teachers. She retired again, after 16 years, realizing that she had been an educator for a total of 50 years! She has been honored with numerous awards. She is all about raising awareness and opening doors. She is all about getting the word out. This is her 22nd book, so far.

ALSO BY DR. SHERRY L. MEINBERG

Bumps in the Night: Fantasy Creatures

Somewhere Out There: Aliens and UFOs

EEUUUW: Animal Gross-Out

An Army of Ants, A Colony of Bats, A Pounce of Cats:
Animal Name Group

WHOA!

A Squirm of Worms

Alzheimer's ABC

In the Nick of Time: Coincidences,
Synchronicities, Dreams, Signs and Symbols

A Cluster of Cancers: A Simple Coping Guide for Patients

Seizing the Teachable Moment

The Cockroach Invasion

Breadcrumbs for Beginners: Following the Writing Trail

Diabetes ABC

Imperfect Weddings Are Best

Recess Is Over! No Nonsense Strategies and Tips
for Student Teachers and New Teachers

It's All Thought! The Science, Psychology, and
Spirituality of Happiness (Teacher's Guide)

Autism ABC

The Bogeyman: Stalking and Its Aftermath
(TV Premier Episode, Investigation Discover (12/12/12)

Toxic Attention: Keeping Save From Stalkers, Abusers, and Intruders

Be the Boss of Your Brain! Take Control of Your Life

Into the Hornet's Nest: An Incredible Look
at Life in an Inner City School

www.ingramcontent.com/pod-product-compliance
Lightning Source LLC
Chambersburg PA
CBHW042339030426
42335CB00030B/3404